COLLABORATIVE ENTREPRENEURSHIP

COLLABORATIVE ENTREPRENEURSHIP

How Communities of Networked

Firms Use Continuous Innovation

to Create Economic Wealth

Raymond E. Miles, Grant Miles, and
Charles C. Snow

STANFORD BUSINESS BOOKS
An imprint of Stanford University Press
Stanford, California 2005

Stanford University Press
Stanford, California

Printed in the United States of America on acid-free, archival-quality paper

Library of Congress Cataloging-in-Publication Data
Miles, Raymond E.
    Collaborative entrepreneurship : how networked firms use continuous
innovation to create economic wealth / Raymond E. Miles, Grant Miles,
and Charles C. Snow.
        p. cm.
    Includes bibliographical references and index.
    ISBN 0-8047-4801-2 (cloth : alk. paper)
    1. Strategic alliances (Business)   2. Entrepreneurship.   3. Technological
innovations—Economic aspects.   4. Corporations—Growth.   I. Miles,
Grant.   II. Snow, Charles C. (Charles Curtis), 1945–   III. Title.
HD69.S8M55 2005
658.4′063—dc22   2005002979

Typeset by G & S Book Services in 10/13.5 Sabon

Original Printing 2005

Last figure below indicates year of this printing:
14   13   12   11   10   09   08   07   06   05

Special discounts for bulk quantities of Stanford Business Books are available
to corporations, professional associations, and other organizations. For details
and discount information, contact the special sales department of Stanford
University Press. Tel: (650) 736-1783, Fax: (650) 736-1784

Contents

Tables and Figures

Tables

Figures

Acknowledgments

In the process of thinking about and discussing the material in this book, and then during the writing and rewriting of the manuscript, the authors have enjoyed collaborating with one another and with various colleagues in academe and business. Although we believe that each of the authors has contributed several original ideas, all of our ideas have been inspired by the thoughts of one another or by one of our colleagues, either in person or in print.

We are particularly grateful to Philipp Käser of the University of Zurich. Philipp offered extensive comments on our manuscript and shared with us his exceptional understanding of collaboration, motivation, and social network theory. We also appreciate comments and suggestions from Kirsimarja Blumqvist, Eric Lindquist, John Mathews, Hector Rocha, and the late Sumantra Ghoshal (we were deeply saddened by his sudden passing while working with us to improve the manuscript). We thank Craig Crossland for locating many of the Web sites listed in the Resource Guide at the end of the book. Lastly, the third author is grateful for the generous financial support of the Mellon Foundation.

We have presented the book's core ideas to several student, managerial, and academic audiences in the United States, Australia, and Sweden. In every instance, we expanded our understanding of the concepts and issues explored in the book. We are grateful for those learning opportunities.

In summary, in all of our interactions associated with the book, people have behaved very much like the participants in OpWin Global Network, the hypothetical organization we discuss throughout the book. Knowledge has been freely and voluntarily shared in the creation of an innovative and, we hope, valuable product. And the entire experience has been thoroughly enjoyable.

COLLABORATIVE ENTREPRENEURSHIP

Foreword

The United States and other advanced economies, virtually all observers now agree, will compete in the twenty-first century at the downstream end of industry value chains. That is, across many different types of industries, firms will succeed to the extent that they can use superior know-how and capabilities to create a continuous stream of innovative products and services for both existing and new customers. Unfortunately, however, most business firms in advanced economies today utilize only a fraction of their innovation potential.

The growing recognition of this problem is driving experiments that, we believe, will result in a new organizational form—a new approach that will allow underutilized resources to be brought to bear on new market opportunities. We call this emerging form the *collaborative multi-firm network*, and it will continue to take shape as forward-thinking managers develop the unique capabilities required to operate it.

We have created an example of such an organization named OpWin Global Network. At the moment, OpWin is a fictional organization that incorporates certain features of today's innovative organizations along with our projections of future organizational strategies, structures, capabilities, and management philosophies and processes. However, we strongly believe that within the next several years, an OpWin-like organization will appear somewhere in the world. Our OpWin originated and is based in the United States, but the first real OpWin may emerge from a region such as northern Europe because, as we explain, conditions there may be more conducive to the growth of this new type of organization. When the first real OpWin appears, wherever that may be, it will evidence powerful collaborative relationships throughout a worldwide network of firms, and it will pursue a business strategy of continuous innovation.

We expect that large firms will be interested in our model as a means of increasing their innovative output and extending their reach, particularly into industries in which they do not already have a presence. We believe that small- and medium-size firms primarily will be interested in joining a multi-firm network because they do not have the resources to engage in continuous innovation by themselves. This scenario leaves the question of leadership open—what types of firms will form a collaborative multi-firm network and lead it to success? We expect the leaders of the new organizational form to be pioneers and risk takers just as past pioneers conceived and designed traditional forms of organizing. And we expect their motivation to be similar, too—pioneering firms will view the collaborative network as an essential means of doing business.

Our vision of a collaborative multi-firm network is admittedly radical but also, we believe, realizable. Our model challenges current business practice in several important ways—it is based on positive human characteristics such as trust and collaboration, it is socially responsible, and it serves all stakeholders because it is so versatile. To convince you, the reader, to seriously consider the need for, and the promise of, this new organizational form, we must introduce new concepts, confront several strongly held business values, and provide credible evidence for why we believe our approach is on target. This is a considerable task, but we hope with this book to facilitate the dialogue and action that must take place in order for a truly innovation-driven organization and economy to become a reality. We invite you to join us in this process.

1   OpWin Global Network

FOR IMMEDIATE RELEASE

January 10, 2010

OpWin Global Network, LLP reported record earnings for 2009. Total earnings for the partnership come from the activities of OpWin member firms and from external licensing fees.

OpWin's performance last year was driven by a continuing flow of new products that found favor across the network's multi-industry global technology markets. New telecommunications hardware, such as the full-color minicam jointly developed by four OpWin firms, was a major success in Asian markets, and the fuel cell output regulator developed in OpWin's Czech sub-network was licensed to both General Motors and Ford.

One of several unanticipated success stories was OpWin's voice-activated software system, originally designed for inventory control, but adapted by a New Zealand member firm for cash-flow management in the Southeast Asian financial services market. Other OpWin products enjoyed similar cross-industry success in communications and bioengineering.

"All in all," said CEO Kristen Morris, "2009 demonstrated once again the power of collaborative research and OpWin's ability to creatively find markets for both new and existing products and services. Our strategy rests on three basic principles: investing in people; supporting a collaborative, entrepreneurial culture; and finding and growing new markets around the world. If we can continue to demonstrate throughout the network that no product or service innovation will be ignored, and that collaboration produces economic as well as psychological benefits, then I see no significant limits to our growth. How are you going to hold back 13,000 entrepreneurs?"

END

CEO Morris later spoke on the radio show *The Day in Business* and began by explaining why OpWin, a limited liability partnership, would make its earnings public. "OpWin strives for open disclosure in all of its activities, including revealing earnings," she noted. "Doing so provides several benefits. It serves as a boost to the stock of those member firms that are publicly held, and it also serves as a promotional tool to attract new members and affiliates to the network. Perhaps most importantly, it allows us to show that an open, collaborative organization can not only survive but also be enormously successful."

The radio show host noted that some business analysts were less optimistic about OpWin Global Network's long-term viability and had expressed concern that OpWin's network of firms was too large and complex to be managed effectively. "It's true," Morris responded, "that to an outsider the network can appear to be uncontrolled, even chaotic at times. But viewed from the inside, it is actually a shifting collection of talent applied to a free-flowing stream of ideas. Both our small and large member firms group and regroup as needed to bring products and services to an array of markets that is constantly expanding. The entire network is a continuous search engine with the capacity to not only design and place a product most anywhere in the world, but to quickly find a way to modify it to make it ever more useful. The firm that originally designed the product may have little if anything to do with its final form or price, but it is confident that it will receive full internal recognition and an equitable financial return. We can't manage this type of operation centrally or even regionally. In the beginning, we developed some broad protocols that define how we maintain our collaborative culture, and we revisit these from time to time. But it's up to the member firms to collectively manage their own interactions."

The show's host also pressed Morris on OpWin's ability to continue its strong record of innovation. The number of patents and copyrights registered by OpWin firms in 2009 was 10 percent above the number for 2008, continuing a five-year upward trend. Intellectual property is fully accessible to network members, and licensing agreements with non-member firms generate a significant amount of OpWin's overall earnings.

"We are as open as we can be," said Morris, "and anyone who can create economic value from what we know should be allowed to do so. What we have tried to do is take the lid off of innovation. Most organizations stifle innovation by forcing it into specific product or service channels—every invention or improvement has to target a specific market. At OpWin, every firm has a standing invitation to adapt any new idea to its own market or to collaborate with another firm, inside or outside the network, to fit it to a jointly developed new market segment. Because everyone knows that ideas are 'generative' rather than competitive, people share ideas across firms, and many an innovation seems to breed two more."

Finally, the radio show host raised the inevitable question of money. Morris had faced this question dozens of times, and it always boiled down to the issue of how member firms could be assured that they would get a financial payoff for their ideas and efforts. "What we have tried to build here," Morris explained, "is a work environment in which people are just as concerned with other people's recognition and rewards as they are with their own. I know that sounds idealistic, but collaborative behavior can be taught and learned just like competitive behavior is taught and learned. First, we continually preach that jointly developed ideas are more powerful than individual ideas. As much as possible, we want people to give credit to their colleagues where appropriate, and we try to explicitly show and communicate how each firm has contributed to a new product at every point along the way. We also ask member firms to think of the long-term aspects of their research and development efforts. Frequently, a new product or service idea has much greater potential return than is apparent from its immediate application. But such returns usually cannot be identified unless our partner firms trust each other and explore the possible benefits of the new idea together. Lastly, even though the firms in our global network offer highly competitive salaries and benefits based on local market conditions, no individual is going to get rich simply by receiving his or her paycheck. Everybody has to be entrepreneurial—to come up with new ideas and to work with other member firms to find customers to buy the new products and services. Each new project is almost like starting a new business—except that the organization and other resources are already in place waiting to be configured and activated. And when the new business eventually begins to pay off, everybody who has been involved must share the rewards equitably."

OpWin Global Network: Vision or Fantasy?

OpWin Global Network is obviously a 2010 projection, not a current reality. Indeed, some of the technological, organizational, and managerial features described or implied in this vision may never materialize. However, there is good reason to believe that the overall configuration of competitive strategy, core capabilities, organization structure, and management processes described in the OpWin example will become visible in various settings at some future date—perhaps in some cases before 2010. Our research over the past two decades, along with our interpretation of how organizations have evolved over the last hundred years, leads us to believe that an organization of networked firms like OpWin is not only inevitable but already under consideration and perhaps even development.[1]

Networks of firms like OpWin will emerge because they are the necessary means of delivering on the twenty-first century's greatest economic promise: the utilization of the world's exploding knowledge base to drive continuous product and service innovations across markets and economies. OpWin is the sort of entrepreneurial engine the global economy is demanding—a knowledge-driven organization that can meet the challenge of continuous wealth creation.

Further, OpWin-like networks of firms will emerge because existing organizations, even those of leading firms, are awash in know-how that is woefully underutilized. For example, estimates by CEOs of the knowledge-utilization rates of even the best-managed companies usually fall in the 15 to 25 percent range.[2] Consequently, a great deal of economic wealth that could be created simply melts away and is seldom regenerated. To succeed in tomorrow's global economy, firms in many industries will want to learn how to quickly create and share knowledge to foster innovation.

Most importantly, a new, powerful multi-firm organization will emerge because visionary managers will create it. They will build and refine this new type of organization just as visionary business executives developed large mass-production firms at the beginning of the twentieth century and just as visionaries in the latter half of that century created network organizations that could rapidly produce customized products and services. Thus, in order to realize the economic promise of the twenty-first century, we believe that the time is ripe for clarifying the organizational efforts of today's pioneering firms and incorporating their accomplishments into a design for the multi-firm network organization of the future.

Barriers Facing the New Network Organization

Entrepreneurial multi-firm networks like OpWin will not emerge naturally or easily. The creation and effective use of continuous-innovation organizations will require a sophisticated model or package of organizational strategy, capability, structure, and process. The new package must tie together an innovation-based market strategy, a new way of organizing human and other resources to support the strategy, and the essential capabilities to make both the strategy and the organization work. And because the package is new and untested, it will be resisted in various ways. Indeed, it will have to overcome enormous barriers to survive just as was the case with every new package of strategy, structure, and capabilities in the past.

To briefly illustrate the difficulty of the task facing the creators of OpWin-like networks, consider three of the many significant challenges facing this new type of organization. First, OpWin as a whole does not have clearly defined product or service lines (though its individual member firms do), and it has even more vaguely defined industries and markets. Its strategy is truly entrepreneurial—to constantly find new combinations of resources that are economically valuable. Such an approach is at odds with existing competitive strategies that usually target known product categories and markets and focus on extracting profits from them. Indeed, entrepreneurship is often thought of as a one-time event—that of starting a new business. The idea of continuous entrepreneurship as a deliberate strategy has yet to be clearly articulated or widely accepted.

Second, OpWin's network organization is complex, and measured by conventional management standards, it is messy. As its

CEO acknowledges, the organization cannot be centrally directed or controlled. Moreover, the core of OpWin's operations depends on the widespread ability to collaborate—vertically and laterally within a particular firm and horizontally across firms in the network. OpWin cannot support its business strategy of market exploration with a traditional organization structure. Instead, the widespread use of collaboration requires a self-managing organization that relies heavily on the competence of member firms as well as ad hoc organization structures specifically developed for each entrepreneurial initiative. Such self-managing organizations are not widely found in today's global economy.

Third, the incentive and reward practices suggested in the OpWin example are not those advocated by today's compensation experts. For example, the currently popular compensation approach of pay for performance requires firms to explicitly identify the outcomes of people's efforts, link the value of those outcomes to the efforts of certain organizational units, and then reward those units for their performance. The basic notion that organization members and network member firms are prepared to share their ideas freely in an effort to generate new knowledge and products without carefully calculating in advance the distribution of returns is contrary to the motivational assumptions of existing economic and management theory. Other theoretical and philosophical barriers also stand in the way of the appearance of OpWin-like organizations.

Despite such challenges, we believe that networks of firms pursuing entrepreneurial strategies sustained by intra- and inter-firm collaborative capability are beginning to emerge. This book anticipates the arrival of such multi-firm collaborative networks, describes how they will operate, and suggests ways to help them take hold and grow.

What This Book Is About

In order for you to fully understand our new organizational model, we must first introduce a few key concepts. The first concept is that of a *package* of resources specifically designed for continuous innovation. A complete package of strategy, structure, capability, and management philosophy and process is needed to succeed. All of the components must be present, and they must be internally aligned with each other and externally aligned to the task of continuous innovation. We will call this package the *collaborative entrepreneurship model*.[3]

Much has been written about the individual components of this package. For example, the successes and failures of corporate efforts to increase knowledge sharing have been chronicled and debated for over ten years, and we now know a great deal about how to develop learning organizations. Discussions of the nature and viability of entrepreneurial strategies, on the other hand, are of much more recent origin. Similarly, collaboration as a means of brainstorming new ideas or resolving conflicts has been studied for as long as fifty years. However, collaborating across firms to first generate and then commercialize knowledge—collaborative entrepreneurship—is just now beginning to be talked about. Overall, what has not yet been clearly laid out and examined is a fully configured collaborative entrepreneurship model: (a) an entrepreneurial strategy that creates economic value through continuous innovation, (b) pursued by a network of self-managing member and affiliate firms, and (c) operated by the essential capability of intra- and inter-firm collaboration.

Another important concept is that of a *meta-capability*—the widespread presence of the knowledge and skills that are crucial to the effective operation of a particular strategy-structure-process package. Each time in business history that a new strategy has been invented, it has required a new organization structure and a new capability essential to its operation.[4] The collaborative entrepreneurship model requires appropriate investments to be made in collaborative capability at several levels—within the firm, within the network of member firms, and even in society itself. Over time, as we know from the development of earlier meta-capabilities, the wealth-creating impact of each new capability is multiplied as it pervades firms and economies. We foresee that, in advanced economies, investments across firms and over time will eventually create a meta-capability of collaboration—a widely distributed social asset that will drive continuous innovation.

A final conceptual challenge is that of describing an expanded *theory of the firm.* The OpWin example imagines a multi-firm network that shares common resources (primarily knowledge) and which, as a total entity, both creates and appropriates economic wealth. The current theory of the firm, a fragmented set of concepts and perspectives emanating largely from the academic disciplines of economics and management, cannot adequately explain or justify this type of organizational arrangement. For example, many management and economic theories quickly lose their usefulness when applied to situations that involve more than a single firm. This is doubly true when those firms band together to pursue strategies based on knowledge and other intangible assets that are difficult to define and measure. Thus, the diffusion of the collaborative entrepreneurship model is being held back, to a very large extent, by theories and institutional practices designed for firms of a previous era.

Beyond the conception of a new type of strategy and organization, this book is about the *practice* of wealth creation and distribution. Once design concepts are clear, the focus switches to issues of implementation and sustainability. Successful firms will put their collaborative entrepreneurship model together with care—they will pay attention to achieving fit among the elements of the model, and they will make heavy investments in the development of essential capabilities. Successful firms will also understand how and why they are successful—they will be learning organizations. Unless an organization learns, it cannot teach, and teaching will be a major means of holding a knowledge-based multi-firm network organization together.[5]

Given that we will be describing how to implement a hypothetical organization, we cannot provide step-by-step instructions for managers to follow. However, we will summarize the lessons learned from the pioneering firms that developed the existing packages of strategy, structure, process, and capability. We will also draw on partial examples of collaborative entrepreneurship by highlighting the relevant features of well-known innovative firms, such as Intel Corporation and Cisco Systems, as well as less familiar organizations such as Technical Computing & Graphics, the worldwide Linux development community, and information technology firms in Finland.

Lastly, we will discuss three examples of large-scale collaboration across organizations: industrial symbiosis in Denmark, partnering in the U.S. civil construction industry, and the global business federation model used by The Acer Group, a Taiwan-based information technology firm. Each of these cases represents one or more of the essential features of an OpWin-like network. Our overall objective is to lay out a path that firms committed to continuous innovation can follow—a path with sufficient examples and evidence to justify meaningful experimentation.

2 The Challenge of Continuous Innovation

Firms that wish to participate in the global economy by pursuing a continuous innovation strategy will have to adopt most if not all of OpWin Global Network's main features. The best way to highlight OpWin's distinctive features is to differentiate its resource package from existing configurations of strategy, structure, capability, and process. This historical discussion will help you to see how organizations have evolved to this point and why existing organizational forms are unable to accommodate a goal of continuous innovation.

As noted in Chapter 1, a package of organizational resources begins with a *business model* (or strategy) that explains how a particular approach will create economic wealth. For example, one firm's business model anticipates creating value by being more efficient than other firms in a given market, while another firm's business model shows how it will add value by appealing specifically to the differing tastes of particular groups of customers in the same market. A complete business model addresses both the present and the future—it shows not only how a firm expects to create wealth but also how it plans to grow its capacity for wealth creation over time.

The second element of every package is an *organizational model* that shows how a firm will assemble, arrange, and manage resources so that the business model can be pursued as planned. Again, one firm may group highly specialized resources around a single value chain, while another firm may organize for greater flexibility and rapid adaptation across several value chains. Obviously, a tight fit between a firm's business model and its organizational model is crucial to the firm's overall success.[1]

A third major component of an organizational resource package is the recognition of the key *capability* required by that particular configuration of business and organization models as well as an understanding of how that capability will be developed and deployed. For example, an efficiency-focused organizational model carrying out a business model of deep market penetration primarily depends on the development of superior forecasting and coordinating capabilities.

Over the past 130 years or so, the period of business history during which all of the modern management approaches have been developed, two basic packages or configurations of strategy, organization, capability, and management process have evolved. Much of the economic success in the advanced economies of the world has clustered around these two models. We refer to these approaches as the *market penetration* strategy and the *market segmentation* strategy. We will describe these tried-and-true strategic approaches and their origins as we contrast and compare them with the resource package that is apparent in the OpWin example.

The OpWin Business Model

The OpWin business model differs from existing business models in that it expects the unexpected. OpWin expects to create and exploit both planned and unplanned innovations. That is, OpWin not only wants to create value by providing new products and services for its existing markets; it also wants to create value from unanticipated product and service ideas that may or may not have value in its existing market(s). OpWin encourages—and seeks to exploit—such innovations by pursuing a strategy that searches for and finds market opportunities for unexpected innovations. It is this explicit focus on capturing wealth outside the boundaries of existing lines of products and services that makes OpWin's business model so entrepreneurial.

Moreover, OpWin's business model is not just entrepreneurial; it is strategically entrepreneurial. A strategy, as noted earlier, is an intent and plan that shows how a firm's resources will be used to sustain economic wealth creation. It is precisely the specification of organizational mechanisms and capabilities for finding markets for unanticipated innovations that makes OpWin's entrepreneurship strategic. Indeed, beyond the existing business models of penetrating or segmenting markets, OpWin's model adds the concept of continuous *exploration* of new markets.

Entrepreneurship and Innovation in Market Penetration Strategies

To some extent, every strategic approach is entrepreneurial, and historically innovation has always played a central role in wealth creation.[2] For example, Henry Ford was behaving entrepreneurially in envisioning an automobile produced at a cost low enough that most people could afford to buy one. Moreover, his Model T car was innovative in its design simplicity, and the assembly-line process that was developed to mass-produce it was innovative, too. However, Ford's creative vision and innovative ideas were both aimed at one product for one market. For the next few decades, Ford Motor Company's business model clearly sought to penetrate and dominate the automobile market through low prices—prices that were generated by cost savings from efficient assembly processes and by economies of scale derived from vertical integration.

Ford's vertically integrated manufacturing process emulated similar steps taken by Andrew Carnegie in the steel industry (and some of Carnegie's ideas came from his prior experience in the railroad industry). In turn, leaders of other firms began applying similar approaches in chemicals and petroleum. Even today one can see the legacy of the market penetration strategy in a firm such as Wal-Mart Stores, Inc. Wal-Mart seeks to dominate one retail market after another, including international markets, by offering a wide array of branded and private-label consumer products at prices lower than its competitors. The firm can offer the lowest prices because its inventory and distribution systems are far more efficient than those of its competitors.

However, while vision and innovation were essential to create the market penetration strategies at Ford, Carnegie Steel (now U.S. Steel), and other leading firms of the time, continuous product and service innovation was the enemy of this business model. That is, the overall success of Ford's mass-production process depended in the early years on limiting product innovation to a single type (and color) of automobile. While products and processes in the automotive, chemical, and retailing industries today are far more diverse and amenable to innovation, unplanned innovations in either products or processes are very costly and are often resisted.

Entrepreneurship and Innovation in Market Segmentation Strategies

Market segmentation strategies, which were developed several decades after penetration strategies, typically incorporated more and different types of innovation. However, as was true of penetration strategies, innovation under the segmentation strategy was typically periodic rather than continuous, and new products and services had to meet demanding corporate hurdle rates in order to cover their R&D costs. General Motors Corporation in the 1920s pioneered the market segmentation strategy in the automobile industry and acted entrepreneurially in adapting its several automotive lines to address market segments of varying tastes and incomes. As opposed to Ford's one-product-fits-all business model, the General Motors strategy was based on "a car for every purse and purpose." GM's multi-product business model called for the sharing of technological innovations and financial capital across product lines located in semi-autonomous operating divisions. Each GM division focused on a single brand of automobile and tailored its various models, features, and prices to its respective market segment.

In a sense, successful market segmentation firms approximated continuous innovation by engaging in "serial" entrepreneurship. While General Motors participated in the automobile market by

TABLE 2-1
Key Features of Old and New Business Models

	Old Models	New Model
Relationship to Market	Penetrate or Segment	Explore
Type of Innovation	Planned, Periodic	Planned, Unplanned, and Continuous
Growth Direction	Vertically and Laterally Within a Given Industry	Horizontal Across Several Industries

focusing its set of divisions on different segments, other firms pursued the same strategy by creating (or buying) new operating units to address segments in their existing markets or in related areas. For example, throughout the 1950s, 1960s, and even into the 1970s, Hewlett-Packard Company literally spun off dozens of new divisions from existing divisions. All of the firm's divisions were related technologically, and to a large extent by managerial philosophy and culture as well (the famous "HP Way"). Hewlett-Packard sought to apply its growing expertise in the research and development of precision scientific measuring instruments to one market after another, creating an ever-growing set of small, collegially managed divisions each of which was focused on applying first-rate engineering and science to a new business market. Thus, each new spin-off division at HP was entrepreneurial—it involved the creation of a new package of strategy, structure, and capabilities to serve a new market. Johnson & Johnson has pursued, for an even longer period, a similar approach across a wide array of markets for health care products and supplies. The firm is one of the world's largest and most diversified makers of medical products. Unlike Hewlett-Packard, which diversified by creating new divisions from existing divisions, J&J primarily used acquisitions to add to its business and product lines and to expand its markets. Each of J&J's subsidiary companies has a great deal of autonomy to run its operation within a well-understood framework of objectives jointly set with corporate management.

Nevertheless, despite their sophisticated capabilities to engage in serial entrepreneurship, neither Hewlett-Packard nor Johnson & Johnson developed a continuous innovation strategy like that of Op-Win Global Network. Table 2-1 summarizes the key features of the business model associated with, respectively, penetration, segmentation, and exploration strategies.

The OpWin Organizational Model

OpWin Global Network is neither large nor small—it is both. In terms of head count and geographic coverage, OpWin is a large organization with approximately thirteen thousand staff spread over many regions of the world. But, viewed differently, OpWin is organized into numerous, mostly small operating units. The network contains approximately sixty firms, the largest of which has slightly more than two thousand employees.

Innovation can originate anywhere within this widely distributed network of firms. Information and ideas are constantly flowing through OpWin's intranet. Whenever a member firm perceives that a particular idea has potential commercial value, that firm can launch the innovation process. Often a virtual team is formed across several member firms that wish to participate in the venture, and its individual members are hooked together by customized computer software. If, in the judgment of the lead team, one or more nonmember network firms should be brought into the venture, then it is that team's responsibility to do due diligence on the temporary new member firm. Such acts of self-organization and self-management occur regularly throughout OpWin.

Indeed, as we noted earlier, OpWin Global Network is a type of organization that does not yet fully exist in the world of business. It is multi-firm, self-organizing and self-managing, adaptable, global, and heavily integrated electronically—and all of these organizational features have been skillfully combined for the purpose of engaging in continuous innovation.

Organizational Models for Market Penetration and Segmentation Strategies

The early market penetration strategy at Ford and the later one at Wal-Mart both depended on the creation of specialized, centralized organization structures, with advanced coordination and control systems and a level of vertical integration that helped to simplify forecasting and planning. While Henry Ford kept his design of the Model T stable in order to keep innovation costs down while maximizing cost savings, Wal-Mart replicated the same regional distribution system and store models in one geographic area after another.

Single-purpose organizational models like that of the early Ford Motor Company and modern Wal-Mart (commonly referred to by economists as U-form or unitary organizations[3]), are built on the notion that individuals and units can pursue specialized tasks if their efforts are brought together by a system of centralized planning, scheduling, and control. The assembly-line worker or machine at Ford can install a single part on every product, provided that the part is scheduled to arrive in proper sequence and at the exact moment it is needed. A Wal-Mart associate can efficiently scan and collect payment for products that have been previously bar coded, delivered, and shelved. However, while new ideas related to every stage of such organizational processes may be valuable innovations, they must be limited in number, as well as carefully planned and implemented, in order not to disrupt current operations.

In contrast to Ford Motor Company, firms such as General Motors, Hewlett-Packard, and Johnson & Johnson organized themselves to address multiple market segments and periodic entry into related markets. Because each market segment (or entirely new market) demanded unique treatment in this strategic approach, each required a set of resources that could be focused on its particular needs, and which could be flexibly and almost independently maneuvered. Chevrolet, Pontiac, Buick, and other GM divisions sometimes drew on common technologies but mostly were allowed to construct processes to shape their car models to fit the preferences and buying power of their targeted customers. GM saw the added cost of some duplication of resources as an appropriate investment to assure market responsiveness.

A similar logic dominated the early multi-divisional (or M-form[4]) organization structure at Hewlett-Packard and, until recently, the group of subsidiary companies at Johnson & Johnson. Customized market responsiveness demanded agile, largely self-directed

TABLE 2-2
Key Features of Old and New Organizational Models

	Old Models	New Model
Type of Structure	Functional, Divisional or Matrix	Network
Number of Associated Firms	One or Few	Several or Many
Type of Management System	Hierarchical (Based on Rules, Planning, and Control)	Self-Managed (Based on Market Factors, Agreed-on Protocols, and Self-Monitoring)

resources even at the expense of some duplication and even with the risks that such actions might entail for the organization as a whole.

Recent organizational developments take into account the fact that even efficiency-oriented firms need to become more adaptive and that market-driven firms must meet increasingly stringent standards of cost effectiveness. For example, the dual-purpose (efficient and effective) matrix organization structure has evolved into the *network* structure whereby a given firm retains its core capabilities and outsources non-core activities to specialist suppliers.[5] A complete network organization contains all of the groups and organizations along the industry value chain—suppliers, partners, and now customers, too. The design and management of a complete multi-firm value chain is commonly referred to as supply chain management, and the best-in-class U.S. company most identified with the supply chain management approach is Dell Computer Corporation. For Dell and other users of this organizational approach, the organization is the entire multi-firm network.

Table 2-2 summarizes the key features of the organizational models that support market penetration, segmentation, and exploration strategies.

OpWin's Essential Capability

At OpWin, there is a belief that "individuals have good ideas, but groups have great ideas." The business press has cited this aphorism numerous times, and indeed it is underpinned by several very real behaviors. For example, the stories and legends that circulate around OpWin tend to be about the outcomes of ideas—how many products were sold, what new markets were opened, which firm had the original idea, and so on. People inside OpWin recognize that successful outcomes occur only after many other people have grabbed an idea and run with it. Of course, the originators of ideas are given appropriate credit, but within OpWin innovative ideas are valued for both their technical and commercial success.

Far more than most organizations, OpWin understands the commercial value of *collaboration*. Knowing that collaborative ability is a key resource of the network, as well as a major source of competitive advantage, member firms are careful to protect and enhance all aspects of the collaborative process. Furthermore, nonmember firms that join the network, either temporarily or permanently, must provide evidence of both their ability to collaborate and their trustworthiness.

Capabilities Required by Market Penetration and Segmentation Strategies

Collaborative ability was not the focus of the early builders of firms following market penetration strategies. Instead, they focused on developing *coordination*. Coordination refers to the ability to bring resources together so that they operate harmoniously. Early in the last century, the developers of scientific management methods began to design various management tools for forecasting, planning, budgeting, and controlling work processes. Over time, those tools have evolved into the sophisticated computer-driven planning, logistics, and control systems that operate modern plants and warehouses, an evolution made possible by the large and continuing investments in training and education by firms, government agencies, and universities. Indeed, this ongoing investment process has resulted in a societal capability, to the point where coordination ability is now a national resource of immense value. Such a widespread meta-capability returns daily dividends for all firms and other types of organizations.

As market segmentation strategies began to develop, it eventually became clear that they not only required effective coordination but another major capability as well. This capability was *delegation.* At General Motors, for example, the early organizational model defined the role of corporate management as essentially that of an investment bank, moving cash to those divisions where it was most needed for profitable growth and expansion. In addition, corporate management was responsible for basic research and development and for transferring technological innovations across divisions. By limiting corporate management's role to these critical functions, GM for the most part left operating decisions to division managers. Corporate and division managers had to discuss and clarify general market boundaries and the approaches each market segment would require, but it was then up to division managers to set and meet objectives. For corporate executives, learning how to limit their hands-on role to that of participating in joint goal setting was truly a challenge.

At Hewlett-Packard, the founders' early commitment to the creation of a "collegial, university-like atmosphere" where "good science could find practical application" made it easy to constrain the growth and control of corporate management and to focus instead on the growth of new divisions—divisions that enjoyed considerable autonomy including control over a generous budget for ongoing research. Similarly, at Johnson & Johnson, growth through the acquisition and decentralized management of subsidiary companies was very much in line with the managerial philosophy of its founder, who trusted subsidiary managers to operate within a well-defined code of conduct (J&J's Credo) that placed high priority on the well-being of customers and employees.

Growth through divisionalization became increasingly common in the U.S. economy during the middle decades of the twentieth century, and authors/consultants—most notably, Peter F. Drucker— helped to clarify the process of delegation used by successful divisionalized firms such as General Motors, Sears, General Electric, IBM, and Prudential Insurance.[6] Management research in the military further enhanced the value of effective delegation, and collegiate schools of business promulgated practices variously called participative management, decentralization, management by objec-

TABLE 2-3

Key Capabilities of Old and New Business Strategies

	Market Penetration	Market Segmentation	Market Exploration
Meta-Capability	Coordination	Delegation	Collaboration
Management Skills	Forecasting Planning Budgeting Controlling	Joint Goal Setting Decentralization Employee Development	Trust Building Protocol Building Project Team Management

tives, and so on. Nevertheless, the evolution of delegation as a pervasive capability followed a rougher path than that of coordination. Indeed, in many multi-divisional firms, delegation was never completely endorsed and practiced, and as a result those (centralized) firms were not very responsive to market conditions and changes.

Table 2-3 summarizes the essential capabilities of coordination, delegation, and collaboration, and their respective association with market penetration, segmentation, and exploration strategies.

Conclusion

Innovation has clearly played a significant role in management and economic development, not only in the U.S. economy but also in every advanced nation. Over the hundred-plus years of modern business history that we just covered, five major types of innovation can be identified:

- product/service (e.g., the invention of the portable computer and online banking),
- market (e.g., entering a new market with existing products or starting a new market with a new product),
- process (e.g., developing a new production or distribution process),
- business model (e.g., direct online sales as an alternative to retail stores), and
- organization (e.g., developing the divisional organization structure or the self-managing team).

Clearly, continuous innovation is *not* the primary focus of either the market penetration or market segmentation strategies. Although the market penetration strategy was built initially on innovative business (large scale for cost reduction) and organizational (U-form) models, the strategy now focuses on occasional process innovations and responds as necessary to the product and/or market innovations of others. Similarly, the market segmentation strategy was quite innovative initially, but it now focuses on limited innovations in products/services and markets.

Therefore, if continuous innovation is to occur, a new resource package must be developed. As previously described, the business model of this new package will focus on market exploration, whereby new markets are developed for both existing and new products. The organization structure that is ideally suited for a strategy of continuous innovation—what we refer to as a *collaborative multi-firm network*—is described in the next chapter.

3   Organizing for Continuous Innovation

Our brief description of how OpWin Global Network is organized to carry out its strategy of continuous innovation portrays organizational structures and processes that are well beyond the experience of most managers. Indeed, most firms today are organized to accommodate only limited, planned innovation. New product or service ideas that fall outside of existing markets are usually suppressed or discarded. In contrast, OpWin is a self-managing network of firms that creates economic value on two main fronts. First, OpWin treats information and ideas from all of its member firms as a common resource to generate product and service innovations for existing markets but also any new markets that can be developed. Second, OpWin's collaborative entrepreneurship model expects its network of firms to develop profitable markets for unanticipated product and service innovations. Thus, while most firms organize to facilitate efficient coordination and control, OpWin's organizational system, a collaborative multi-firm network, creates value through complexity—an approach that defies traditional management thinking.

As in the previous chapter, a comparison of OpWin's approach to more familiar organizational forms is probably the best way to explore its unique features. Organizations today typically attempt to develop and apply their know-how outside their existing product and service lines either by acquiring new business units or by forming alliances with other firms to share product-market ideas and information. OpWin's dynamic, horizontal network of firms shares some features with each of these approaches, but it exhibits some additional features as well.

Creating and Acquiring New Business Units to Spark Innovation

As we noted in Chapter 2, traditional firms such as Hewlett-Packard and Johnson & Johnson carried their innovative know-how into new markets by creating divisions or acquiring new business units. Because each division or business unit was semi-autonomous, it could focus its resources on a particular market without day-to-day supervision by corporate officials. New ideas that did not fit the markets of existing divisions could be used to spawn a new division through a process whereby higher management authorized the formation of a new business unit. As long as the new division provided an appropriate return on the parent firm's investment, while not interfering with the customers of other divisions, the corporation could continue to exploit its know-how by moving into new areas.

However, growth by sequential divisionalization is not a strategy for continuous innovation. Divisionalization is not designed to exploit both planned and unanticipated innovations wherever they may arise and wherever they may lead. Instead, the creation or acquisition of a new business unit is an important, costly, and time-consuming event, one for which most firms plan carefully and undertake only periodically. Moreover, despite efforts to focus division resources on distinct markets or market segments, product and service lines may gradually spill over into the domains of other divisions, presenting higher-level managers with disputes that are difficult to resolve. Lastly, as divisions multiply, redundancies, whether real or imagined, also multiply. Many firms with multiple divisions begin to centralize support functions at the corporate level, and these firms face the constant temptation to centrally coordinate innovation across product lines and markets in the hope of achieving scale economies in sales, manufacturing, and research and development.

In a further attempt to avoid redundancy, progressive firms of earlier decades began to use cross-functional business teams to accelerate and streamline innovation without the need to create completely new divisions. In its appliance division, the General Electric Company honed the process of new product development through the use of product teams that learned to take ideas from the design stage to the production stage in a matter of months. Today, Intel Corporation has continued to improve its use of project teams in the development of each succeeding microprocessor design. Indeed, Intel's organization accommodates overlapping teams so that the production of the current microprocessor model can proceed efficiently while a new model is being designed, tested, and readied for production. At that time, the production and sale of the preceding model is wound down to a profitable halt.

While the various matrix structures used by GE, Intel, and other firms are more efficient than creating autonomous new business units, they are not designed for continuous innovation. They, too, are intended for planned, sequential innovation. Moreover, because matrix mechanisms are centrally planned and coordinated, they leave little room for even that level of unanticipated innovation that may occur within the autonomous division. In short, the more innovation is managed, the narrower and less spontaneous it becomes.

Clearly, OpWin's organization structure has some features in common with the divisional and matrix forms. For example, its multi-firm network looks a bit like the multi-divisional forms at Johnson & Johnson and at Hewlett-Packard in previous decades, in the sense that there is a headquarters group and operating units (member firms) that have considerable autonomy. However, OpWin's individual member firms are completely autonomous, and they choose to associate with the OpWin network because it is in their self-interest to do so. Indeed, member firms are not only responsible for their own profitability; they are free to withdraw from the network after giving six months' notice and satisfying their current inter-firm projects and obligations. This independence is essential to assure that each firm can operate without corporate constraints and is motivated to use its own resources to maximum advantage. Perhaps even more important, the fact that OpWin member firms are truly independent means that they are responsible for managing their own relationships with their fellow firms.

The ability to self-manage inter-firm relationships is the key to OpWin's ability to create and capture economic value from innovative ideas that would be lost in most divisional and matrix organizations. Inter-divisional rivalry for capital and for performance-based rewards usually results in limited product-service development across division lines, and often motivates divisions to resist sharing ideas that might be valuable in the markets of other divisions. Corporate attempts to induce divisions to freely share information and to cooperate in systemwide projects frequently produce limited results. Inter-unit collaboration, when it occurs, is often the result of voluntary actions among divisional groups or projects initiated by corporate knowledge managers that temporarily suspend incentives for inter-divisional rivalry. However, unauthorized and/or bootlegged collaborative efforts are, by definition, not part of everyday firm or inter-firm practice and tend to be narrow, fragile, and difficult to sustain or grow over time.

Innovating Through Inter-Firm Alliances

Innovation outside of a firm's boundaries can and does occur through various types of alliances involving two or more organizations. Innovation-focused alliances are regularly created to share research and development resources, particularly in fast-moving industries such as biotechnology, nanotechnology, and computer software. Indeed, in rapidly evolving technical areas, it is difficult for any firm to be able to develop and allocate innovation resources across all potential product-service markets.

Most contractual alliances are focused on a specific objective. Common alliance designs call for sharing research and development facilities and/or personnel, the creation of cross-firm marketing and/or design task forces, and joint efforts to establish common standards for key interface designs and specifications that will facilitate innovation and reduce design redundancies. Alliance goals are often narrow because the firms involved are concerned with gaining the benefits from cooperation and shared resources while carefully protecting their current market positions and preventing the inadvertent sharing of intellectual property outside of the alliance's scope. Indeed, many alliances are short-lived because while firms see the benefits of shared information and resources, they develop concerns that their alliance partners may be gaining a disproportionate share of the technical or market benefits. Thus, for many firms, being forced to depend on trust and relational experience rather than measurable contractual obligations tends to inhibit vigorous alliance participation.

Historically, some firms have been especially adept at finding ways to create economic value across firm boundaries. For example, Corning Incorporated has gained widespread recognition for its myriad alliances.[1] Early on, Corning established a dominant research position in the ceramic sciences, and it usually had more innovation capability than it could profitably develop and apply in its existing markets. Such underutilized capability motivated Corning to seek partners to help it create economic value from product research and development outside of its own marketplace, and the firm presented attractive opportunities to potential partners to engage in joint ventures or licensing agreements. Over time, Corning created a reputation for trustworthiness and creativity in alliance building that gave it a growing outlet for its research and development expertise. In a period where most organizations managed their know-how to fit their own markets, Corning exploited its capacity for innovation by forming long-lasting joint ventures and other types of alliances.

During the 1980s and 1990s, many firms, especially those in high-technology industries, pursued innovation strategies by creating internal venture capital processes.[2] Corporate-supported investment committees were set up to fund product-service innovations that fell outside existing market boundaries. Their intention was to facilitate promising innovations that were unlikely to proceed through normal development channels and to find a home for the resulting products and services either inside or outside the firm. The venture capital committee helped to create internal alliances across units or to facilitate the spin-off of an innovation through licensing, a joint venture, or the creation of a new, independent entity. While there have been numerous successes from utilizing the internal venturing approach,[3] it is not yet clear that firms are using it to fully exploit their capacity for innovation.

Some firms have formed alliances with their key customers. For example, 3M has organized a lead user idea-generation process in which the firm selects, funds, creates, and markets new products in collaboration with lead users. The 3M lead-user process even offers tool kits that allow users themselves to improve products.[4]

Recently, high-technology firms, especially Intel Corporation and Cisco Systems, have begun a process that cuts across both alliance and internal venture capital approaches. Innovation and growth through acquisition has long been a tradition in the high-technology sector. Larger firms acquire smaller firms whose technological innovations can be incorporated into the larger firm's products and services—in effect, the big firms simply buy a large portion of their research and development. Other firms expand their reach horizontally and find broader application for their technological know-how by acquiring smaller firms in related technologies and markets.

Intel and other hi-tech firms, however, have gone beyond these approaches by taking ownership positions in small downstream firms that may at some point become markets for the upstream firm's future products. Intel is particularly motivated to explore potential outlets for its microprocessor design capability, which already far exceeds its application in existing computer markets. Intel's informed guess is that microprocessors will become commonplace in a wide variety of products, and it wants to use its equity positions in small firms to help it search out the most promising markets. Alliances, joint ventures, and acquisitions are expected to follow those exploratory investments.

Organizing for Continuous Innovation

OpWin's horizontal network of firms also shares some features of the alliance approach to innovation. OpWin's member firms collaborate across firm lines, sharing common knowledge to create and exploit economic value through innovation. However, OpWin's knowledge and information sharing is broad and general-purpose. That is, neither the resources (knowledge and information) that are shared, nor the purpose for which they are shared (continuous innovation), is constrained. Instead, the expectation is that OpWin's member firms will share product-market ideas and perhaps even tangible assets in order to turn potential innovations into revenue-producing realities. As noted earlier, ideas born in one firm may be expanded and developed in a second firm and taken to market by or with a third firm.[5]

OpWin Global Network is designed to exploit the know-how and capabilities of all of its members and to do so without the constraints of central planning or prespecified limits. To some extent, OpWin's network shares some features of another form of network organizing, the industry value chain.[6] Since the 1980s, firms in a wide range of industries have learned how to cut market-response time and improve resource utilization by creating vertical networks of firms along the value chain. Beginning in industries such as book publishing, used on a global basis in automobiles and athletic footwear, and taken to new heights in the computer industry, value chain networks are now commonplace. In such networks, firms with downstream skills in distribution and marketing connect to upstream firms with skills in manufacturing and assembly, and together they optimize the use of their resources—a process that has been referred to as virtual integration. Just as Wal-Mart assists its upstream suppliers with information to guide their manufacturing and supply schedules, Dell Computer Corporation shares information and creates relationships with upstream suppliers of components and software so that Dell can supply customized computer models at ever lower prices.[7] Information sharing and cooperative relationships have increased the efficiency of many value chain networks to the point where product and process innovations are constantly expanding to the benefit of both upstream and downstream partners.

However, compared with OpWin's expectations, even the most advanced value chain networks are too restrictive. OpWin's interactions across its member firms flow in every direction and are shaped and reshaped as needed to carry innovations through to the

TABLE 3-1
Comparison of Periodic and Continuous Innovation Processes

Planned, Periodic Innovation	Unplanned, Continuous Innovation
Primarily Targeted at Existing Markets	Primarily Targeted at New Markets
Internal Use of Business Teams and Venture Capital Processes	Broad, General-Purpose Alliances Among Independent Firms
External Use of Acquisitions and Special-Purpose Alliances	Multiple Role Playing (R&D, Marketing, etc.) by Some Firms Across Different Projects

market. At any given time, a particular OpWin firm may be operating at more than one point along several industry value chains. It may, for example, be playing an R&D role in one value chain and a marketing role in another. Further, some of the value chains may cut across traditional industry lines. Thus, OpWin Global Network is dynamic both vertically and horizontally, and no member firm is forced to occupy only a single value chain position over an extended period of time.

Such complex, dynamic relationships do not imply that OpWin's resources are unfocused or stretched too thin. Indeed, for considerable periods of time, any given member firm may be engaged primarily in designing, producing, and/or marketing a limited set of products and services, and this firm may have organized a stable network of external suppliers and distributors. All of these activities may be highly focused and, at that moment, may be the most creative and profitable use of that firm's know-how. The difference is that OpWin's firms are free to shift directions, using a portion of their resources to pursue ideas and innovations on their own or with other firms as opportunities arise. By making certain that what they are doing and discovering are visible across the entire OpWin network, member firms are always potential innovation suppliers, users, and/or development partners.

Table 3-1 summarizes the main features of OpWin's continuous innovation approach and compares them to the periodic innovation approach.

Collaboration: The Key to Success

Clearly, OpWin's way of organizing is a far more ambitious mechanism for producing innovation than commonly used approaches such as acquisitions, spin-offs, cross-functional business teams, alliances, and value chain networks. Therefore, shouldn't we expect OpWin to fall victim to the same sorts of management maladies that afflict those approaches? Why, for example, don't OpWin's member firms protect their own know-how just as do divisions or subsidiaries? Why aren't OpWin's alliances with other firms limited in scope and prone to only short-term success? Why don't larger OpWin firms acquire their smaller partners so that they can control knowledge development and make the innovation process more efficient? These are reasonable questions given what we know about how existing organizations work.

We believe that the OpWin network is less susceptible to these kinds of problems not because its business model of market exploration is too new to be evaluated, or that its organizational model of a dynamic, horizontal network of firms is infallible, but because the entire system is driven by a crucial capability. That capability is collaboration. OpWin's member firms are different because they collaborate in creating innovation, and, equally important, they collaborate in capturing and distributing the returns to innovation. The capability to collaborate in the creation, appropriation, and distribution of economic wealth is neither well understood by, nor widely found among, today's firms. In the next chapter, we will discuss the process of collaboration in detail, and we will provide different examples of how collaboration has been used for commercial purposes.

4 Collaboration: The Essential Meta-Capability

We have continually referred to OpWin as a collaborative network of independent firms, and we have argued that collaboration is the essential capability that allows OpWin to effectively operate its unique type of organization. We believe that the widespread ability to collaborate among OpWin's member firms is the main reason that this particular network has held together rather than succumbed to the self-serving behaviors that hamper or doom so many other alliances. Therefore, in this chapter we want to define and clarify the concept of collaboration—to clearly show why it is vitally important to the effective operation of a multi-firm network focused on continuous innovation. In the process, we will differentiate collaboration from other related concepts, specifically, cooperation, competition, and the more recent hybrid concept of co-opetition.

Our discussion will focus not only on the surface differences among competitive, cooperative, and collaborative behaviors but also on two important underlying factors: the *motivation* that energizes each type of behavior and the *beliefs*, especially the level of trust and commitment, required to sustain behavior. Collaboration is a sophisticated behavior that can be learned, but its underlying motives must be clearly understood and unfailingly accepted for it to work.

The Competitive Standard

OpWin's independent member firms share information and knowledge that may be used by any other member firm without specific permission, and they often commit resources to inter-firm projects whose full returns can only be calculated after the fact. This is not how most managers have been taught, either in their formal education or through everyday experience, to behave.

Indeed, most firms view their know-how as a proprietary asset and the primary means by which they create economic value in the marketplace. Managers have learned that protecting that know-how is how a firm defends its competitive position. And competition—between firms and among units and individuals within firms—is the conceptual centerpiece of much of the global economy, a position justified by the expectation that vigorous competitive behavior will result in the most desirable economic outcomes.[1]

Of course, managers and firms seldom engage in totally unconstrained competition. In many mature industries, leading firms realize that price competition sometimes follows a difficult-to-control and perhaps mutually destructive path, one that can be avoided with a little judicious restraint and some careful signaling and testing. Economists call this phenomenon "mutual forbearance," the tendency for firms to avoid acting aggressively if they believe that their competitors will retaliate. Moreover, firms frequently avoid direct price-based competition by focusing on market segments that can best be served by a particular package of know-how and other resources that is different from that of their competitors. Such a differentiation strategy results in indirect competition that is not particularly bothersome to firms in the industry.[2]

Firms learn to accommodate competitive pressures with a strategy that maximizes the utilization of their particular mix of resources while not encouraging damaging attacks from other firms. And, inside firms, operating units and individuals learn similar behaviors and achieve similar outcomes. Indeed, while reward systems inside many modern firms encourage competitive behaviors among units and individuals, organization members learn over time where and how to compete as well as where and how to cooperate—to act in some mutually beneficial level of consort, whether openly acknowledged or subtly demonstrated. Nevertheless, being careful—and calculating when, where, and with whom to share information—is an unquestioned part of most managers' beliefs.

Motivation in competitive situations

Competitive behavior is driven by participants' desires to achieve as large a share of the rewards available in a given situation as their energy and abilities will allow. This motivational assumption is explicit in economic theory (individuals and firms act in their own self-interest), and a focus on competition as the best means to achieve goals and rewards is reinforced by the speeches and writings of leaders in business, politics, and sports.

Of course, the philosophy of competition emphasizes more than just the attainment of goals and rewards. Business leaders also encourage managers and employees to find satisfaction in the work they do as well as in the rewards they receive, and coaches and other sports figures challenge players to enjoy the game for its own sake while still focusing on the goal of winning. Politicians assure voters that maintaining an economy's competitive edge is essential to assure "the good life" for the citizenry. Nevertheless, the primary motivational driver in competitive situations is the quest for an external target such as a promotion, a team championship, an increase in market share taken from a competitor, and so on.

When the primary purpose of an activity is the reward it will bring, psychologists refer to the underlying motivation as extrinsic—the reward comes from a source external to the doer. On the other hand, the athlete who gives his or her best effort even when there is little if any hope for team or individual prizes is said to be motivated intrinsically, that is, by the sheer feeling and satisfaction of playing. Similarly, some managers and employees are recognized by coworkers as persons who "love what they do" and would "do what they do even if they weren't being paid for it." Such people are intrinsically motivated by their jobs.[3] While few activities are undertaken purely for either their intrinsic or extrinsic rewards, the primary form of motivation that drives an individual is important in differentiating among competitive, cooperative, and collaborative behaviors.

Trust in competitive settings

Participants in most settings, from business to sports to politics, expect other participants to learn and follow at least some basic rules of the game. Those who don't are quickly spotted as people who are not to be trusted. Unfortunately, cheaters can and do win, at least in the short run, and therefore the level of trust that exists among participants in competitive situations is an important determinant of how they behave in those situations. The minimum level of trust that most organization members expect of their superiors is that they will apply sanctions as specified in the rules (both the organization's rules and general moral and ethical principles). A higher level of trust exists when superiors can be counted on to allocate rewards in a similarly fair and principled manner. In short, most organization members in competitive situations seek sufficient trust to assure that at least basic rules and traditions will be followed.[4] We will return to this point repeatedly as we discuss cooperative and collaborative behaviors.

One final comment on motivation and trust is important, however. It concerns when and to what extent a participant calculates his or her motivation and trust. In competitive situations, participants are assumed to calculate the returns they expect from their striving from beginning to end. Similarly, trust in competitive situations is often calculated in advance, especially when participants have had little if any experience with one another. Such calculation is required before participants can determine how they should and will behave in a particular encounter. However, repeated interactions can provide a level of trust that lessens the need for deliberate, ongoing calculation.

Cooperation

To some extent, the behavior within and across OpWin's network of firms can be understood using the familiar concept of cooperation, defined as working together for a common purpose. However, two individuals or parties can work together while primarily serving their own or the other party's interests. This motivational distinction, we believe, is the main difference between cooperation and collaboration (which will be discussed below).[5]

Typically, cooperative behavior is first explored in early childhood. For example, with help from parents and teachers many children learn that their own toy can be turned into two or three toys by sharing. Of course, children also learn that not everyone has fully internalized the message of cooperation or behaves consistently. As people mature, they have various opportunities to explore the costs and benefits of cooperative behavior, and most people develop some ongoing associations at work or in their community or neighborhood where cooperative behavior is expected and enjoyed. In those familiar settings, there is the expectation, though not always carefully measured, that everyone benefits from cooperative behavior.

Whereas cooperative behavior in most cases rests on some amount of testing and calibration,[6] some organizations appear to be more like OpWin in that their members simply expect other members to share information and ideas freely. To a significant extent, OpWin-like expectations exist in universities and other scientific or professional organizations. Such expectations are built on the collegial values of open sharing of ideas and information and the careful acknowledgment of their sources. Indeed, most members of such communities are there because they find the process of generating and sharing ideas exciting and rewarding—they are, for the most part, intrinsically motivated.

As we noted in Chapter 2, it was exactly this sort of collegial sharing of ideas, information, and excitement that William Hewlett and David Packard sought to take from their university experience into the business world. However, the early ideals of Hewlett and Packard, as later HP executives lamented, did not always hold up under the heavy pressures of sharing resources, rewards, and recognition within and across fifty or more divisions. The observation by HP executives that collegial cooperation became more difficult as the firm's size and markets grew raises the question of how scientific and professional communities maintain such behaviors as their organizations and management challenges grow in size and complexity. The answer, in part, is that collegiality is sustained by widely understood *protocols*, such as the attribution of sources of ideas, the citation of earlier research and findings, and the careful socialization of new members into the community.

In academic communities, membership is usually attained through doctoral programs where much learning occurs from mentoring and apprentice-like service as a junior colleague. While those relationships often produce valuable research findings and create the excitement of learning and achievement, their role in the academic socialization process is equally important. Junior colleagues learn values, norms, and expectations from their senior colleagues, and they pass them along to their own doctoral students. The academic profession invests time, training, and other resources in the development of the collegial value of information sharing because it realizes the importance of this value to the continued operation and effectiveness of the profession.

Similarly, in the early days at Hewlett-Packard, collegial values were learned in a university-like environment. Engineers designed and sold products to customers who, in most cases, were also technically trained—scientists and engineers designed products for other scientists and engineers. Moreover, the expectation was that the firm would compete by designing and building the best product, one that was distinguished by its technical excellence, and by getting it to the market ahead of other firms. Members enjoyed the process and outcomes of the scientific endeavor, and the firm reinforced that satisfaction by returning a sizable portion of each unit's earnings to fund that unit's ongoing research and development efforts. Thus, the underlying motivation among many HP employees in the 1950s and 1960s was similar to that in many universities and scientific communities: the excitement that comes from acquiring, sharing, and creatively advancing knowledge.

However, as HP grew, more and more products were being produced for business and consumer markets that were concerned primarily with cost, reliability, and compatibility rather than sheer computing power or engineering brilliance. Moreover, competitive pressures forced increasing attention to total firm profitability and prompted frequent comparisons of performance across and within divisions. Collegiality, under these conditions, tends to give way to a concern for unit and individual rewards, and motivation becomes more extrinsic than intrinsic. Similarly, the trust that once allowed ideas to be shared freely within and across HP divisions came under pressure. Individuals and units were motivated to become more calculating and protective of their own ideas and information. Under such circumstances, the growing concerns of senior HP managers about the demise of collegial behavior probably should have been more widely anticipated.

Co-opetition

Whereas investment in the development of collegial values is intended to reduce the need for *a priori* calculation of returns from cooperative information and idea sharing, a more recent approach called *co-opetition* (simultaneous cooperation and competition) sets out to make such calculations both more explicit and accurate.[7] The advocates of co-opetition argue that the true maximization of total benefit occurs when firms cooperate in the generation of wealth (creating the pie) while still competing for their own share of the enhanced outcome (dividing the pie). The idea that the sharing of information, ideas, and resources will lead to the creation of a larger economic pie is also a pillar supporting OpWin's strategy. However, this is as far as the similarity goes.

From a game theoretic perspective, co-opetition is simply the rigorous search for mutually advantageous agreements that lead to a higher total potential gain for both parties. Strategies following co-opetition principles rely on complementary value-adding behaviors such as, for example, those between Microsoft and Intel or those between credit card companies and airline mileage programs. Such programs benefit two or more parties without constraining their individual efforts to obtain maximum returns. Similar strategies have been used in other settings involving bidding, negotiations, and customer and supplier relationships. Game theory principles and techniques have also been used to analyze and calculate the costs and benefits of alternative competitive and cooperative relationships.[8]

Although the capability to engage successfully in co-opetitive relationships is interesting and challenging in its own right, the key point from our perspective is that co-opetition strategies highlight similarities in the underlying motives of both competitive and cooperative behavior. That is, in either a competitive or cooperative approach, the primary outcome that each participant is pursuing is an improvement of its own position. The impact of the joint behavior on the current or potential partners is secondary. Viewed from this perspective, every cooperative action, from toy sharing to neighborhood ride sharing to business participation in community programs to a firm sharing information with its suppliers, is meaningful primarily because of its usefulness in helping the participants achieve something they value. Put another way, co-opetition is behavior that is extrinsically motivated, highly calculative, and mostly self-serving.

Collaboration

Collaboration, like cooperation, can be defined as a process whereby two or more parties work with each other to achieve mutually beneficial outcomes. Collaboration can be directed toward any mutually desired objective: solving a problem, resolving a conflict, creating a new business, and so on. Our concept of collaborative entrepreneurship is that of a *joint enterprise*—the creation of something of economic value based on new, jointly created ideas or knowledge.[9]

Continuing our focus on the motives and beliefs of interacting participants, we suggest that collaboration differs from competition and cooperation in two main ways. First, cooperation is motivated by the benefits each party expects to receive from sharing ideas, information, or resources. Therefore, while cooperative behavior may be enjoyable in its own right, it is primarily extrinsically motivated. Second, because cooperative behavior ultimately involves the pursuit of self-interest, it requires periodic or even continual assessment by each participant of the amount of trust and commitment of the other party. In collaborative relationships, on the other hand, each party is as committed to the other's interests as it is to its own, and this commitment reduces the need for the continual assessment of trust and its implications for how rewards will be divided. Because it is the innovation-generating relationship itself that is valued,

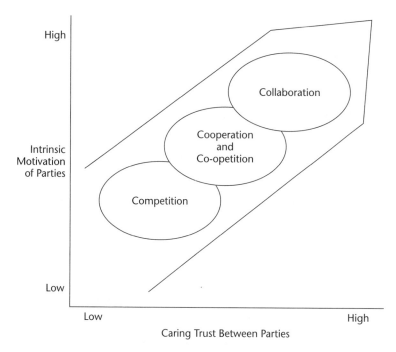

FIGURE **4-1**   Knowledge Sharing Potential of Competition, Cooperation, Co-opetition, and Collaboration

collaborators can focus on its intrinsic aspects knowing full well that future returns will be equitably allocated. Thus, a collaborative relationship is built on intrinsic motivation and caring trust.[10] Figure 4-1 illustrates how collaboration has a higher potential for knowledge sharing than either competition or cooperation.

Because collaboration is not primarily self-serving, its goals and methods are sometimes difficult to define and accept, even when we observe the behavior firsthand. Thus, the boss who acknowledges a subordinate's contribution as more important than his or her own, the researcher who demands equal recognition for all project members, and the athlete who publicly signals a teammate's assistance may be viewed with a mixture of admiration and suspicion. Their behavior is not what we expected and therefore we wonder if they are secretly self-serving and manipulative.

Among the participants themselves, however, the dynamics of collaboration are often very powerful. The freedom to contribute without having to calculate one's return is empowering. Ideas can be offered without reservation, knowing that they will be recognized and treated with respect. The contributions of others can be gratefully accepted and acknowledged without worrying about the immediate payoff. The opportunity to work together and build on a constantly growing stream of creativity is exciting and satisfying. It is not uncommon for people to remember their involvement in collaborative endeavors as among their most enjoyable experiences.

Nevertheless, although collaborative behavior occurs all around us—in families, among friends, within teams at work and play, across organizations, and among colleagues in the same professional community—collaboration is not a widely understood or valued phenomenon.[11] Moreover, while those who have engaged in collaborative activity often treasure its memory, they may not always advocate collaboration for others.

Motivation to collaborate

Because of the shared belief that equitable (fair) outcomes will always be pursued, collaboration does not require continuous cost-benefit calculations. If collaborative partners constantly assess the value of the information and ideas they are sharing, then they will inhibit their own ability to contribute fully and creatively. Thus, to join and continue in a collaborative relationship, one must find the interaction satisfying in itself without concern for the ultimate outcome.

However, a participant's willingness to suspend *a priori* calculation needs to be supported and reinforced over time. The actions and statements of collaborative partners are essential to this process. If members continue to demonstrate their commitment to the well-being and recognition of everyone involved, and if they engage in a sincere and productive search for the equitable distribution of any gains resulting from the collaborative effort, collaborative relationships can be deepened and sustained. Indeed, the achievement of equity by an equal distribution of gains is a difficult if not impossible undertaking and is neither essential nor even expected. What *is* essential is a demonstrated long-term commitment to the concept of equitable rewards and the widespread belief that equitable distribution will always be sought.[12]

In truly collaborative interactions, it is the recipient of an idea who takes pleasure in acknowledging its source, and it is every member's concern for the interests of everyone that is the source of collaborative freedom. Collaborative relationships among peers usually build on the willingness of one or more parties to invest in the clear recognition of another's contribution. Honest praise for another's idea or other contribution can, over time, become the norm within a work team or among peers interacting across units. Collaboration becomes more effective when more experienced peers respond to praise by making certain that less experienced peers learn to use their own capabilities.

Collaboration in Large Organizations

The examples we have used to define and illustrate collaborative behavior and its motivational and trust dynamics have, for ease of presentation, been limited to pairs of individuals and teams, and to larger groups of professional people. However, our hypothetical OpWin Global Network is a large commercial enterprise organized as an international network of firms. Are there any real organizations that have similar commercial goals and that rely heavily on collaborative behavior to pursue them?

The Linux development community

One large organization built primarily on a collaborative foundation is the Linux open-source network.[13] Linus Torwalds, who sought to create a mechanism for designing, extending, and supporting a global computer operating system, began the Linux community. Torwalds reasoned that ownership concerns and the competition for rewards based on proprietary intellectual property constrained the pace of development in existing computer operating systems and reduced their overall power and potential. Torwalds decided to make the Linux kernel, the core of its system, a commonly owned asset available for development by anyone prepared to support and contribute to its evolution. Over the years, the Linux operating system has been increasingly used by engineers and scientists, incorporated into high-powered servers, and most recently utilized to power an inexpensive computer capable of running Windows software.

The most noteworthy features of the Linux community are that it is open and voluntary. Anyone can use the Linux operating system, as long as they do not attempt to make it proprietary. Firms can incorporate the system into their products for free as long as they pass along the savings to consumers. The purpose in keeping the system open is to make it everyone's property and thus to make its development everyone's responsibility.

The appeal of the Linux operating system to the dedicated computing community is enormous. The original system was quickly developed, debugged, and expanded, and growing legions of users around the world continue to add to its development. Development or project teams focus on various system and application programs. Membership in those groups is highly prized but achieved only after demonstrating the skills, commitment, and a firm grasp of the Linux value system. Linux values are very similar to those of a professional discipline. Membership is earned by demonstrated competence and maintained by learning and following accepted protocols. Participants in the Linux development community (called contributors and maintainers) submit proposed improvements for public review and carefully recognize the sources of their ideas and the contributions of former and current contributors.[14] Because these behaviors are voluntary and undertaken for their own sake, Linux participants seldom if ever step outside expected behavioral boundaries. Their behavior demonstrates their own trustworthiness as well as trust in their fellow Linux participants.

Of course, most Linux participants enter the network with a motivational mind-set that is well suited to collaborative behavior. They frequently come from technical and scientific communities, are highly motivated by technical problems, and are excited by the task of creating and modifying computer software and fixing problems. Because they are volunteers, they are self-selected and can only be directed by a self-managing organization. Participants' motivation is almost entirely intrinsic, and they are prepared to trust others with similar values and mind-sets.

Linux's voluntary, self-managing global network of contributors and maintainers has defied most predictions concerning the limits and quality of their technological development efforts. Many Linux users claim the system is more reliable than others available commercially, and Linux is fast becoming a dominant computer operating system. Its incorporation into both high- and low-end products signifies its scope, and its many supporters include leaders in the computer industry. We believe the Linux example provides evidence for the notion that a very large group of people can work together to develop a commercially successful product without being part of a single firm.

Communities of practice or creation

Firms such as Sun Microsystems, Caterpillar, and Fiat are experimenting with processes that shift the locus of innovation beyond the boundaries of the firm, to a community of individuals and firms that collaborate to create joint intellectual property. These experimental approaches aimed at broadening the source of innovation, as well as accelerating its pace, have been called "communities of practice" or "communities of creation."[15] In organizational terms, the community of creation model seeks to strike a workable balance between order and chaos. The model recognizes that most innovative ideas are the product of a joint process, so incentives must be created for outsiders to offer their ideas and expertise. At the same time, however, the sponsoring firm does not want to be overwhelmed by new knowledge and information, nor does it want to lose control of the intellectual property rights that are jointly created. The experiments that have been conducted so far indicate that the development of a community of creation requires:

 – a common interest,
 – a sense of belonging,
 – an explicit economic purpose,
 – a sponsor,

- a shared language,

- ground rules for participation,

- mechanisms to manage intellectual property rights,

- physical support of the sponsor, and

- cooperation as a key success factor.

We believe that the various communities of creation that exist today demonstrate that it is possible for a group or firm to lead a process of continuous product-service innovation by designing a collaborative organization that has certain identifiable features and processes.

Finnish information technology firms

Although the Linux community is quite large, it is not a formal organization. Conversely, the community of creation model is more formalized, but it tends to take shape around the contours of existing industries. To find large-scale examples of firms engaging in sophisticated collaborative behavior, one might turn to the growing information technology industry in Finland.[16] The Finnish IT industry is an increasingly visible producer of global patents, products, and systems. With the exception of Nokia and a few other firms, the approximately six thousand Finnish IT firms tend to be quite small, though they now account for roughly 10 percent of Finland's exports and are one of the largest contributors to total Finnish R&D expenditures.

Given the sizes of Finnish IT firms, it is not surprising that alliances and partnerships are common. Large firms need the technology developed by small firms, and small firms need the financial muscle and distribution power of the large firms. Nokia, it is estimated, has over three hundred major partnerships in its domestic network. Another estimate is that 49 percent of all small Finnish IT firms have alliance relationships, and fully two-thirds of all small firms already have alliances or expect to have them. The Finnish experience is not unique, in that alliances abound in the United States and are growing in number in Taiwan, India, and other countries.[17]

However, Finland's size, culture, and the rapid emergence of its information technology industry have given it some notable features.

A recent study of the industry spotlights the role of *fast trust* in helping to create and sustain partnership networks.[18] Because Finnish firms are competing in a global marketplace with larger and more powerful competitors, they must match and even lead technological progress without the size or resources of the global giants. They can do so only by creating and supporting networks as complex as Nokia's. They must find and develop collaborative relationships with a host of smaller firms for every major project and must sustain those relationships for future use. And they must do so without damaging the creativity or motivation of their smaller partners. It is in this context that both large and small firms describe the value of fast trust—the quick evaluation and appreciation of a partner's trustworthiness.

Although it is not clear precisely how fast trust is demonstrated, it appears that trustworthiness can be determined fairly quickly by direct interaction, reputation, and reference checks with other firms. A firm's behavior and its reputation for trustworthiness thus become resources for attracting valuable partnerships, and its ongoing support for that reputation can be viewed as a continuing investment. Fast trust is the basis for suspending the need for *a priori* calculations of collaboratively generated returns, and it frees collaborators to exchange ideas and information willingly, assured by their joint commitment to pursue an equitable distribution of rewards.

Perhaps a study that highlights trust and collaboration in Finland should not be surprising. The Finnish society is among the most egalitarian in the world—the difference between the income of the top 20 percent of the population and the bottom 20 percent is among the lowest of developed countries. Moreover, Finnish citizens have come to expect high-quality public education and good pay to complement government-provided health care and retirement benefits. Traditionally, Finnish managers do not expect to receive compensation far in excess of that received by their employees, and wealth is not widely and aggressively pursued in a generally

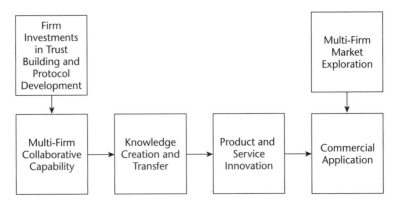

FIGURE **4-2**   Relationships Among Collaboration, Knowledge Sharing, and Innovation

well-off society that is highly educated and cosmopolitan. Entrepreneurship and capitalism are clearly becoming ingrained in Finland, however, so it may be that collaboration for commercial purposes is facilitated by certain prior societal conditions.[19]

The examples of Linux, communities of creation, and Finnish information technology firms all indicate that continuous innovation is feasible. Also, all three cases suggest that individuals and firms that are able to work together collaboratively can achieve continuous innovation. Figure 4-2 shows the relationships among collaboration, knowledge sharing, and innovation.

Conclusion

As the preceding discussion suggests, collaboration is not yet a well-developed or widespread capability in most organizations. It is an essential element, however, in the free sharing of ideas necessary for continuous innovation across a multi-firm network.[20] Perhaps most important in this regard is the freedom from the *a priori* calculations of returns that collaboration brings. Believing in the trust and commitment of all parties, and recognizing the intrinsic motivation driving their behaviors, participants can exchange knowledge and ideas at a level well beyond what is possible with competition, cooperation, or co-opetition.

Turning collaboration into a meta-capability shared across firms and throughout society will require significant changes and investments at the firm and societal levels, a topic that we will return to in Chapters 8 and 9. It is our belief, however, that there is currently enough collaborative potential in the world of organizations for us to imagine how a multi-firm collaborative network should be designed and managed.[21] In the next chapter, we provide those details for OpWin Global Network.

5   **The Complete Collaborative
     Entrepreneurship Model**

To this point, we have provided an impressionistic view of the OpWin Global Network and its principal components. We have laid out an architect's sketch of how an entrepreneurially powered business model, supported by a dynamic multi-firm network organization and a rich mix of intra- and inter-firm collaborative capabilities, can create economic wealth through continuous innovation. Now it is time to provide a more detailed picture—to add the engineer's blueprint to the architect's sketch.

The detailed blueprint shows how multi-firm networks like OpWin are designed and managed. Although such networks are not yet present in the global economy, we believe they are coming. We also believe that their operating mechanisms can be anticipated, primarily because those features will come from existing organizations, though they will be packaged in a new way. In this chapter, we identify those mechanisms and describe how they fit together. In the process, we seek to answer the kinds of questions that will naturally arise about this new way of organizing. For example, what types of firms should be in the network, and how should they be assembled? Can some firms be temporarily affiliated with the network instead of being a full-time member? What is the role of a central services office in a continuous-innovation network? How can an open catalog of ideas, information, and projects be created to serve member firms?

What do individuals and teams do in an organization such as this? How can the entire global system be sustained?

Today's organizational designers can choose from among several basic structures and forms of governance. Some of OpWin's features, for example, resemble those that are common in partnerships and alliances. Others appear to be borrowed from voluntary organizations, consortia, and trade associations. Many aspects of Op-Win, as we have been describing it in previous chapters, are extensions of the network form of organizing that has been honed over the past two decades.

Thus, as we unroll OpWin's design blueprint, we are offering only one organizational option from among the several that could be drawn. Indeed, we suspect that the complete and polished designs adopted by future OpWin-like organizations will be superior to the design outlined here. Nevertheless, we will try to support our claim that OpWin is a realizable vision—an organization that, with sufficient commitment and investment, can be constructed from currently available forms of strategy, structure, and governance.

Organizational Components and Structure

Figure 5-1 shows OpWin's major components, all of which we have introduced earlier as examples, including its form of ownership, network of member and affiliate firms, and the Central Services Office.

OpWin's form of ownership

OpWin's origin can be traced to a small, innovative computer chip design firm in Silicon Valley (call it Chip Design, Inc.). As a contract manufacturer, Chip Design's business is to design next-generation chips and computer software for user firms in various industries. One of Chip Design's key customers is in the home appliance industry, where it manufactures various types of appliances for use in smart homes—homes with many automated features—and certain kinds of commercial settings. The appliance firm had provided the bulk of Chip Design's business for several years, but Chip

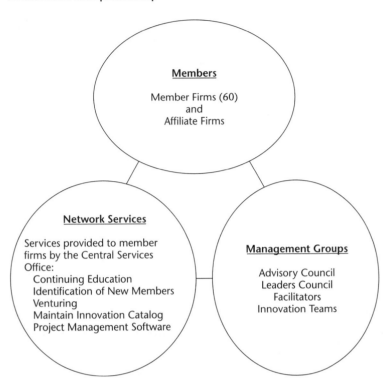

FIGURE **5-1**   OpWin's Network Organization

Design's leaders realized that at some point the rate of innovation in integrated appliance systems probably would slow down. They realized, too, that Chip Design's focus had always been on the technical side of computer systems, not in locating new customers.

These realizations came as an unpleasant surprise to Chip Design's management group. Because the firm's core competence was in R&D, and not in the identification of product applications and customers, it became starkly apparent to management how fragile Chip Design's business model was. Chip Design's managers shared their concerns with leaders of the appliance company, and together they began to plot a vision and plan for Chip Design that would be more sustainable than its present business approach. The most notable result of several brainstorming sessions was the idea that computer chips might have a promising application in high-end children's toys such as robots, machines, and video games. Chip Design approached a well-known children's toy firm, and over the next few years, the two firms worked closely together on the creation of several successful toy lines.

One could argue that OpWin Global Network was born during this period. Chip Design saw that it needed an organizational model that would allow it to innovate on a continuous basis, and it also knew that it could not pursue an innovation-oriented business strategy with only a few customers. Therefore, the three firms—Chip Design and the appliance and toy producers—joined forces in a limited liability partnership (OpWin Global Network, LLP). They decided to name the new organization OpWin Global Network to call attention to their proposed mode of operation: OpWin for an open window into the capabilities of the system, Global because they envisioned having member firms from around the world, and Network because firms could be flexibly linked to each other to work on a particular project or new line of business. It took several more years for OpWin to begin to attract interest among potential member firms, but after a dozen or so companies had joined the partnership, OpWin was able to refine its management system into an approach that drew praise from the business press and created the momentum needed to grow the organization.

Member and affiliate firms

OpWin is a dynamic network of member firms and their temporary affiliates. The network is dynamic in that none of its members has a fixed role, and the resources each firm has assembled are often shared in business ventures with other firms, usually but not always within the network. It is also dynamic in that its membership has expanded dramatically since its founding, and the process of adding new members is ongoing.

Each member firm joined OpWin as a profitable independent entity, and it is each firm's responsibility to maintain its ability to support and grow its own resources and to generate significant income for itself and for its network partners. Firms vary in size from less than a hundred staff members to a few thousand, and each firm is expected to serve all of its stakeholders in an exemplary manner, in line with OpWin's stated pledge to set the highest standards of customer satisfaction, human resource management, and natural environment sustainability. Each member firm measures its own (a) net wealth creation, (b) human resource growth and retention (including educational and skill upgrades of staff), and (c) annual customer satisfaction, and members send this information to Op-Win's Central Services Office.

Member firms are expected to create products and services for their own markets and to work with other firms in the network on innovation projects. Within their own markets, firms pursue organic growth through market penetration with existing products or services while attempting to meet the expectation that at least half of their revenues will be generated by continuous innovation. Innovations in a given firm's market come not only from ideas and efforts within the firm but also from the continuous scanning of ideas and innovations from other network firms. Each firm describes product ideas, development projects, and product-service upgrades in Op-Win's *Innovation Catalog*, an electronic database accessible only by member firms. Not only do member firms post potential value-generating information in the catalog; they are also expected to proactively contact other firms that might have an interest in their ideas, projects, or new models.

Firms in related markets regularly send design, marketing, and operating staff to OpWin's *Market Exploration Workshops* that are held periodically. Moreover, firms also collaborate across the network on development projects that do not have obvious connections to their own markets. Staff specialists may be invited by another member firm to visit and discuss a listed idea or project, and they may in turn request additional meetings to provide elaboration and possibly joint pursuit of an idea or project. In some instances, a staff member from Firm A may work with Firm B on a particular project even though it has been determined not to have relevance in Firm A's usual market. When this occurs, Firm B pays for the staff member's time and effort. Further, if the contributions from Firm A are later incorporated into a profitable product or service, Firm B is expected to provide an appropriate return for Firm A such as a royalty or one-time payment.

In all cases, firms are expected to engage in joint development efforts and to contribute needed skills and abilities to other firms without prior calculation of costs or benefits. It is the responsibility of the user to recognize contributions and initiate equitable payment, and to make certain that the provider is satisfied with the outcome. On joint projects, it is the market owner's responsibility to propose a schedule of returns that is seen as equitable by its project partner(s). Where new or shared markets are served by a jointly designed product or service, the participating parties draw lots in advance to determine which firm will take the lead in proposing market-delivery responsibility and an equitable distribution of returns.

The heavy focus of OpWin firms on continuous innovation often limits their interest in taking an active role in creating wealth via the long-term production of goods or services. In those cases, OpWin firms work with outside partners to produce components or even complete products for OpWin markets. After assuring the market success of a product or service, OpWin firms may license designs to outside partners for their own longer-term sales and service. Licensees, too, are required to meet OpWin's customer satisfaction and environmental standards.

To become a member of OpWin, a firm must demonstrate its *competence* and *trustworthiness*. This can often be achieved by the successful completion of a single project. At any point, a firm can apply for membership, which must be voted on by all members after an OpWin review team has assembled a sponsorship document. Alternatively, a firm may be affiliated with OpWin on a temporary or infrequent basis, typically as a licensee or other type of contractual provider.

In summary, OpWin member firms operate independently in their own markets and in alliances of one sort or another with members of the network to design and take to market a continuous stream of innovative products and services. However, OpWin's alliances differ from other alliances in several important ways. First, OpWin alliances are usually generated by ideas and activities that are viewed as open—available to all member firms, with users responsible for acknowledging the source of the ideas and the contributions of their partners. Also, OpWin alliances are open-ended rather than special-purpose, and rewards are determined after the fact rather than in advance. Lastly, roles, responsibilities, and returns are governed not so much by contracts (though these are widely used) as by norms of equity and collegiality, aided by an agreed-on set of explicit operating *protocols* (such as user responsibility for provider equity and satisfaction).

As noted earlier, the concept of ideas and information as an open source, available to all firms in the network, bears a resemblance to the concept of openness that governs the Linux development community, where users throughout the world contribute to and utilize that computer operating system without payment or charge. Contributions to the operating system and its application programs are widely cited and recognized by community members. There is, however, one key difference. The Linux system is viewed as a tool to create economic wealth, not the product itself, and is therefore treated as a free good by all parties. Conversely, OpWin's shared ideas are themselves wealth generating, and the expectation is that returns from the innovation process will be equitably shared among the firms involved.

Central Services Office

The Central Services Office (CSO), which is located at Chip Design, Inc.'s facilities, is different from the typical corporate headquarters office. Because OpWin firms are independent and self-managing, the term *central office* carries no connotations of ownership or hierarchy. Indeed, virtually all of the activities performed by OpWin CEO Kristen Morris and her staff are viewed as support services for the network's member firms. The services provided have evolved over time, designed jointly by Morris and various leaders of member firms. No new practices are initiated without approval from the OpWin Advisory Council, a twelve-person group of OpWin member-firm executives who serve two-year staggered terms, and no new service or system is put into place until all member firms have signed off on it.

The services provided by the CSO fall into five categories (see Figure 5-1). The first type of service is *continuing education*, and it focuses mainly on the development of collaborative skills and processes. The CSO facilitates discussions of inter-firm collaboration among member and affiliate firms, and it publishes accounts of outstanding examples of wealth creation and appropriation.

In line with this responsibility, the CSO conducts an orientation and training program for the managers and staff of new member firms brought into the OpWin network. This intensive program focuses on OpWin's protocols for idea recognition and sharing, and for the equitable distribution of rewards. Numerous examples of these protocols are shared, and incoming members analyze cases and engage in role-playing to develop a deep understanding of, and commitment to, OpWin's way of doing business. The orientation process includes discussions with other member firms and planned collaborative learning opportunities.

Because OpWin's collaborative capability is viewed as its most important asset, the role of the CSO in promoting continuous collaborative learning is its number-one priority. Every major collaborative venture, whether a success or failure, is analyzed for its learning content, and particularly instructive cases are written up and distributed to member firms.

The Central Services Office, working closely with member firms, is also responsible for *identifying new network members*. The CSO staff helps member firms create visionary scenarios for their respective industries, including market maps that identify potential new OpWin members. New network members are sought for their knowledge and expertise in either (or both) product/service R&D or marketing. On the input side, OpWin's efforts are similar in many ways to firms such as Cisco Systems that scan across industries for the possible acquisition of firms that create promising new technologies. On the output side, OpWin's efforts resemble those of Intel Corporation, which is constantly scanning for start-up firms in the computer and communications industries that might create new microprocessor applications or markets. Intel then invests in those firms whose work appears to be aligned with Intel's.[1] However, there is one key difference between OpWin's search process and those of firms such as Cisco and Intel—OpWin is looking for new, independent network partners, not acquisition or investment candidates.

The third category of services for which the CSO is responsible is *venturing*. The CSO provides a variety of venturing services to member firms, such as facilitating the acquisition of patents for new processes and designs. CSO staff specialists work with member firms on all matters involving the pursuit and protection of intellectual property (patents, copyrights, trademarks, etc.), and they lead the search for firms outside OpWin that might want to license a particular new product or design. CSO involvement in the licensing process can take one of two main forms. The first approach is where one or more member firms are seeking a licensee for a specific product or service. In this case, the CSO staff helps the member firm(s) locate an appropriate partner and facilitates the formulation of the licensing agreement. The other approach is more proactive. The CSO staff is continually looking for external firms that might make use of ideas in the *Innovation Catalog* but have not yet drawn the attention of member firms. In such cases, the licensing opportunities uncovered by CSO staff are first presented to member firms to ensure that there are no conflicts with their plans. If no conflicts are present, the CSO arranges a licensing agreement on its own, providing a percentage of the licensing fee to the member firm(s) that originated the product or design idea.

OpWin's licensing process is widely recognized in the corporate world as both creative and equitable, and many firms outside the OpWin marketplace have learned to inspect OpWin's existing inventory of products and services for potential applications in their own markets. OpWin treats potential affiliate members with the same respect shown to member firms, and as a result, former and current licensees regularly recommend new venture partners. Licensing fees typically represent 15 to 25 percent of the revenues of member firms and serve as the primary source of revenue for the CSO.

CSO's fourth service responsibility, and one of its most important, is to maintain and improve the *Innovation Catalog*. Here the overall objective is to make ideas, product or service designs, and research projects developed in any one firm available to all member firms. The *Innovation Catalog* is on OpWin's intranet and is entered through a secure portal.[2]

The format of the catalog, and the processes for its use, are designed to be interactive and personal. A powerful search engine that is regularly upgraded leads the way. Each item in the catalog is clearly described, including its status regarding copyright or patent protection, and each lists a contact person. Most initial contacts are made by e-mail or telephone and are followed up with face-to-face meetings as needed. A versatile software program permits secure interactions across multiple network partners who are interested in the development of a particular idea, product, or process.

Most multi-unit technology firms have well-developed intranet systems to facilitate idea and information exchange. The main difference between those systems and OpWin's is that the *Innovation Catalog* is actually used. In the typical firm, organizational units are careful to control their own intellectual property, and sharing is usually limited. Efforts to create knowledge directories are common, as are their failures. OpWin members, on the other hand, freely share ideas because they know that they cannot reap the full economic harvest from their creativity without collaborative partners, and they are confident that their contributions will be equitably rewarded.

The final type of service provided by the CSO is *project management*. The CSO does not manage any of OpWin's various projects directly; this is done by the member firms themselves. However, the CSO houses the electronic project management and accounting system, a sophisticated computer software program developed by NetAge, Inc. A consulting firm that specializes in knowledge management, NetAge helps firms set up and operate virtual organizations that may span firms, industries, and countries.[3]

OpWin's project management software has been designed for use on its intranet. The lead firm on a new project, with the CSO's help, will open its own project site. This site is given a project name, and the member and affiliate firms that are collaborating on the project have secure access to the site. It is the responsibility of the lead firm to enter all operating data on a timely basis so that project partners can monitor costs and progress. The accounting data contained on the site are the basis for the final distribution of rewards among partners and for a summary accounting statement of the project if requested by a customer.

Management Processes

The cast of characters at OpWin—network member and affiliate firms, the Central Services Office, and potential venture partners—have well-understood roles to play in a constantly evolving, largely self-managing process. However, there are three guiding principles that make OpWin both efficient and effective as a dynamic multi-firm network organization: (1) the use of operating *protocols* instead of hierarchical controls, (2) a philosophy of *minimal organization*, and (3) the *self-management* of teams and firms.

Operating protocols

OpWin's three pioneer firms began using the term *protocol* to differentiate voluntarily agreed-on behaviors from procedures that in most companies are formulated, imposed, and enforced hierarchically. For example, in international diplomacy or labor-management collective bargaining, protocols help participants search for solutions to problems or conflicts by specifying widely accepted criteria and processes that reduce the possibility of offence and promote integrity. Within the corporate world, OpWin was inspired by Johnson & Johnson's well-known Credo and by Ritz-Carlton Hotel Company's Gold Standards. Both of these public documents take corporate values and translate them into specific actions and priorities that are clearly communicated to organization members. Such actions and priorities are consistently used in both companies for decision-making purposes and for guiding everyday employee behavior.

OpWin's pioneers discussed and codified the three general behaviors that they believe are most likely to lead to trust and collaborative behavior: (1) demonstrate trust by immediately sharing something valuable, (2) stimulate equitable reciprocity by volunteering a generous distribution of jointly created returns, and (3) publicly give credit to collaborators for their contributions to innovation projects. Over the years, the Central Services Office has illustrated these key operating protocols in case studies written by CSO staff. Examples of the protocols in use cover situations in member and affiliate firms as well as in customers' firms and surrounding communities. The original protocols have spawned subsequent practices such as the concept of idea users initiating proposals for the distribution of returns and the *Innovation Catalog*'s tracing and acknowledgment of the sources of ideas.

Today, new OpWin member firms learn the "OpWin Way" in an orientation program built almost entirely on the three original operating protocols. Newcomers read written cases about the protocols and their supporting behavioral dynamics, and they see how protocols are put into practice in short video clips filmed in actual member firms. Newcomers may also be asked to write up their own experiences, especially if they involve particularly vivid successes or failures.

In summary, the early decision to use (positive) principles rather than (negative) rules to guide organizational behavior has given OpWin a powerful, flexible set of guidelines for collaboration and self-management.

Philosophy of minimal organization

OpWin's organization design is based largely on the philosophy of Technical Computing & Graphics, a group of innovative information technology firms based in Sydney. The TCG Group, composed of thirteen small firms with a total staff of approximately two hundred, believes that an organization, like any support service, should help firms to pursue their strategies and to do their work. For example, TCG refers to its R&D approach as triangulation, since it involves relationships among three types of firms: (1) an outside joint venture partner, (2) a large firm that will be the principal customer, and (3) one or more TCG firms that will voluntarily collaborate on the new project. Each new initiative begins with the creation of a project organization led by a TCG firm and composed of its internal and external partners. Nothing in the way of organizational or managerial mechanisms will be added to this basic triangular structure unless the parties involved believe that it is necessary.[4]

OpWin similarly tries to keep organizational constraints to a minimum. The network's philosophy is that the organization should work for its member firms, not the other way around. Although Op-Win's network includes approximately sixty independent firms, each of which has its own structure and management systems, the network itself has only three levels, capped by the previously mentioned Advisory Council. Its basic structure is a *Leaders Council* at the executive level, *facilitators* at the managerial level, and *innovation teams* at the operating level (see Figure 5-1).

Leaders Council members are appointed by the Advisory Council to staggered terms based on technical and/or market knowledge as well as collaborative skills. The Leaders Council meets periodically in the United States or Europe to assess all of the ongoing projects and to offer assistance as appropriate. Because most activities are carried out by self-managed innovation teams, middle-level managers at the member firms facilitate operations at the request of teams and keep the Leaders Council informed of project progress, possible spin-off ventures, and team needs for equipment and technical assistance. Team members carry out production tasks or work with suppliers to produce goods or services. They are also responsible for writing up ideas, working with facilitators (and perhaps Leaders Council members) to hone designs, and scanning the *Innovation Catalog* for related information and projects. Facilitators help to enter materials in the catalog, and they participate in innovation discussions with the facilitators of innovation teams in other firms. As previously described, all information such as customer orders, production schedules, materials requests, and accounting data are available to any member firm on the project management database.

Self-management

At OpWin, innovation teams are largely self-managed. The use of self-managing teams within firms is not new, and OpWin's practices are in many ways similar to those of Kyocera and other leading firms in team management. What is different at OpWin is the extent to which teams are also self-managing across firms and with customers and suppliers. Every OpWin team is empowered to make certain that customers are treated fairly and efficiently. Each team maintains its own customer satisfaction data. Team members are fully aware of, and responsible for, recording all of the costs of their product's production and delivery in the project management database, and they are responsible for maintaining the minimum expected net profit margin of 12 percent for OpWin's member firms. Customers are made aware of OpWin's various profit margins and are thus assured that they are not being exploited. Indeed, new customers can, and often do, request a complete accounting statement from OpWin. However, most ongoing customers simply rely on OpWin's word and reputation.

Team members are expected to think about other OpWin firms as they develop their own technologies, products, or markets. Teams are excited to see their ideas chosen from the *Innovation Catalog* and are eager to collaborate on inter-firm projects. They self-schedule to accommodate their own operating requirements, keeping customer needs at the top of their priorities, while collaborating with teams from other firms. Facilitators help to locate resources within and outside the firm as needed, and they are expected to be able to answer team members' questions about how OpWin operates. To the fullest possible extent, OpWin teams are their own managers, as their bosses merely assist them in meeting their own goals and objectives.

Sustaining Mechanisms

OpWin seeks to maintain its historical performance levels, as well as strive for future growth and improvement, through its motivation and reward practices and its ongoing investments in intangible asset development.

Motivation and rewards

OpWin permits individuals and teams in its member firms to satisfy their needs for personal growth and accomplishment primarily through the work that they do, coupled with the confidence that their economic returns will be equitable and their long-term rewards will be exemplary. All OpWin firms are expected to pay wages and salaries at the upper tier of the market, with generous benefits including support for continuing education. In less developed economies, OpWin's wages and salaries typically exceed local levels, brought up by OpWin's international reach and standards. OpWin firms are urged to work with local leaders to make valued contributions to the communities in which they operate. All OpWin firms must provide their staff with resources, such as computers and training, which they need to coordinate their activities within the global network.

Regarding long-term rewards, OpWin maintains a systemwide defined benefits retirement program, including health care benefits. Both employee and member firm contributions, along with a contribution from OpWin out of its licensing fees, fund this plan. Also, member firm employees receive periodic grants of performance-based stock shares in their own firm, which are fully vested after five years. OpWin firms also match employee contributions, up to the maximum allowable percent of their salaries, to purchase shares of their own firms, which are held in trust for five years and then become fully vested.

Each OpWin member firm is a partner in OpWin Global Network, LLP. New members must buy into the partnership, though they are allowed to pay their fees over time. Originally, OpWin firms also paid an annual operating fee of five percent of gross revenues to cover the costs of the staff and activities of the Central Services Office, but the revenue from licensing now covers all of those costs and generates a significant profit of its own. The OpWin partnership agreement mandates that at least 50 percent of net earnings be returned to members, with the remainder being used to expand the services of the CSO and to create a fund that member firms can borrow from to develop new projects.

Overall, OpWin's reward system is designed to offer short-term pay and benefits at levels high enough to cover member needs generously and long-term payoffs that have a substantial potential upside. This system allows OpWin member firms to pursue innovation collaboratively without the need to constantly calculate their own returns. Thus, collaborative projects are conducted primarily for the enjoyment of creating new and valuable products and services.

Ongoing investments

There is broad recognition within OpWin that the entire enterprise is built primarily on *intangible assets*. Therefore, investments made by member firms in areas such as R&D, education and training, information technology, brand development, and relational capital are calculated on an annual basis and reported to the member firms by the Central Services Office. Raw data are compiled at each member firm using a measurement tool called VAIC (Value Added Intellectual Coefficient), and the portion of each investment attributable to OpWin's business is determined. This information is then sent to the CSO for aggregation and dissemination. By using the VAIC system, OpWin is able to keep track of its accumulating value as an organization, and each member firm can see where investments are being made by its partners.[5]

One of OpWin's most valuable assets is its stock of trust. To assure trust, all accounting data are available to any member firm, and summary financial statements are available to suppliers and customers. The cost of this open system is viewed as a continuing investment in trust. Similarly, ongoing training in collaborative skills is viewed as an investment, and OpWin is pleased to include personnel from affiliate firms and public organizations in its training and development programs.

Building and maintaining trust demands complete openness and the willingness to listen and respond to concerns immediately and fully. Over time, members learn that they are expected to exercise responsible self-management and control and that, in turn, they can expect the same from every other member. Members also learn that they can make mistakes without retribution. What they cannot do, however, is breach the trust that has been placed in them. Doing so will become rapidly known throughout OpWin, and the negative effect on future collaborations serves as a powerful deterrent of opportunistic behavior.

Trust is built by risk taking. OpWin takes risks by sharing information and ideas openly and widely—member firms could violate this trust, as could individuals. OpWin takes risks in its generous licensing arrangements—for example, the risk that the license will turn out to be underpriced in terms of the value it brings to the licensee. OpWin takes risks with its reliance on self-management— teams can waste time, effort, and resources, and they have opportunities to behave in their own self-interest rather than in the overall interest of OpWin. These are real risks that occasion real costs from time to time. However, OpWin is built on the belief that with sufficient investment, including the assumption and management of risk, trust can be built, sustained, and used as a resource in collaborative endeavors.

Conclusion

We have laid out a detailed blueprint of how a multi-firm collaborative network such as OpWin can be built and operated. Each of OpWin's major components has at least one real-world counterpart, and some have several existing forms. For example, OpWin's ownership structure is not dissimilar to that of global partnerships in professional services such as consulting, accounting, and legal. Similarly, self-managed teams can be found in many firms around the world. OpWin's *Innovation Catalog* is an enhanced, and more workable, model of the early knowledge-management directories found at a number of firms. Inter-firm cooperation is widespread and could, with the proper modifications and investments, be transformed into full-blown collaboration across both firms and industries.

In our view, there are two main lessons that can be drawn from this description of OpWin. First, such an organization could be constructed right now using components, processes, and philosophies that already exist. Our blueprint provides only one of several possible options. Second, creating an OpWin-like organization requires continuing investments and the willingness to take risks that are substantial. However, while OpWin is still a vision, real collaborative alliances exist today that suggest that OpWin's fictional achievements indeed may be realistic. In the next chapter, we present three case studies of such multi-organizational collaboration.

6   From Vision to Reality

Case Studies of Multi-Organizational
Collaboration

As mentioned in Chapter 3, many firms began in the 1980s to incorporate their lead customers and suppliers into their own decision-making processes. The primary goal was to create a customer-driven organization that delivered desired products and services to customers on a consistent and timely basis. Such customer-driven firms also began to solicit and use the opinions and suggestions of their main suppliers. Here the main goals were to reduce costs and increase efficiency. For example, BMW, the automobile manufacturer, collected customer opinions about all of its models through focus groups and surveys. It also invited its main supplier of car seats to participate in the design process so that the resulting seat designs were not only customer-friendly but also efficiently manufactured and delivered. Similarly, in a more elaborate process, General Electric created its Work-Out! program in which GE managers, customers, and suppliers meet and discuss ways to improve the entire value chain for each of GE's businesses.

Customer-driven firms learned from these types of programs that they could increase customer satisfaction with their product and service offerings by working collaboratively with their value chain partners. Not only could collaborative efforts all along the value chain lead to process improvements and faster response times, but they also could lead to enhanced product innovation. Supplier know-how could be incorporated into downstream firms' designs, and downstream firms' expertise and user feedback could be communicated to upstream firms to improve both process and product designs. As such, supply chain relationships often proved to be fertile ground for growing collaborative competence.

Nevertheless, learned collaborative capability exercised along the value chain is limited by the market opportunities recognized or uncovered by the supply chain's downstream firms. Useful product and process ideas will still be abandoned if they do not readily fit the supply chain's existing purpose.

It is our intent in this chapter to explore the collaborative process in applications that lie outside the typical value chain. Three examples of multi-organizational collaboration have gained international attention not only because their processes are different from those normally seen in the business world but also because they are successful. The first example is an industrial-municipal alliance in Kalundborg, Denmark, which has been referred to as "industrial symbiosis."[1] The second example is a partnering process used in the U.S. civil construction industry on many large-scale projects that jointly involve the public and private sectors.[2] The final example comes from the Acer Group, a Taiwan-based information technology firm that has worldwide operations organized as a federation of businesses.[3]

Moreover, each of these real-world examples appears to have evolved in much the same way as our fictional OpWin example. At OpWin, an initial positive outcome from a collaborative relationship encouraged two firms to broaden the relationship to include a third firm. That broadened alliance not only flourished, but it also taught its members about the power that accrues from the shared ownership and application of a growing body of technical, managerial, and organizational know-how. Over time, OpWin's vision became a teachable strategy for wealth creation through continuous innovation. At present, OpWin fully understands its capabilities, and it supports and expands them with targeted investments in organizational and intellectual assets.

In this chapter, we describe the dynamics of the three real-world examples of industrial symbiosis, partnering, and business federation, showing how their evolution and approach support our collaborative entrepreneurship model. In each example, we point out the specific aspects of collaboration that we believe extends to OpWin.

Industrial Symbiosis in Kalundborg, Denmark

Beginning in the early 1990s, the small Danish city of Kalundborg has been the site of an evolving, successful program of industrial-municipal collaboration that its participants refer to as a "non-project" run by a "non-organization." As of 2003, this non-project has created financial returns of over $200 million on an investment of approximately $90 million—an average annual return of over 16 percent. Though difficult to quantify, it has also produced returns in terms of regional identity and pride that can be used as the basis for further economic development.

The source of these returns is annual savings from symbiotic exchanges across a network of municipal agencies and private businesses. For example, heat generated by various factory processes is used without cost by other organizations, as are excess power and other industrial by-products. Firms involved range from producers of electricity and petroleum products to producers of insulin and enzymes. All told, there are nineteen different exchanges involving water, energy, and waste products. In addition to these hard projects, there are a number of soft projects where collaboration has focused on sharing store and laboratory capacity, creating common contracts with external entrepreneurs, and developing useful personnel arrangements such as flexible hours for spouses. The eco-industrial park in Kalundborg is one of the most internationally well-known examples of a local network for exchanging waste products among industrial producers, and in the future it may serve as the primary model for cities to jointly shape industrial development and environmental sustainability.

Such symbiotic outcomes are the result of collaboration among a growing list of participating organizations. Various deals have been creatively constructed and voluntarily struck. All of the involved parties engage in self-directed and self-controlled actions without a common owner or managing hierarchy. As the projects have multiplied, the parties have developed not only trust among themselves but also substantial collaborative expertise, a graphic though limited example of the evolution of a shared meta-capability. The development of that expertise is today the subject of municipal pride as well as a desire to gain a better understanding of the factors that have contributed to the experiment's success.

For our purposes, the Kalundborg experience has returns far beyond the valuable outcomes that have been produced by this industrial-municipal alliance. In our view, an equally important outcome is the evidence that a voluntary, self-directed experiment can lead to the growth of a continuing and expanding collaborative search for creative value-adding approaches to utilizing resources. Perhaps most instructive is that the hierarchically managed firms in Kalundborg, as well as the municipality itself, recognize that the success of this alliance is based primarily on collaborative behavior. Building on that understanding, current participants invite and encourage broadened participation, but they recognize that they can only teach and facilitate collaboration, not direct or manage it.[4]

In management terms, the Kalundborg experience illustrates an OpWin-like progression from experiment to understanding to growing the network of participants.[5] This is an example of organizational learning—participating organizations come to recognize the value of collaboration and then begin to use it to an increasing extent. Nevertheless, industrial symbiosis in Kalundborg is only a single case involving a small number of geographically proximate organizations. Moreover, Denmark's social statistics look less like those of the United States and more like those of Finland, where our earlier example of collaboration among information technology firms suggested that the ability to collaborate might have a cultural basis.

The question that should now be addressed is whether there are examples of collaborative problem solving and innovation among organizations in a different region and cultural context, particularly cases where collaboration has been expanded and sustained. The answer, we believe, is yes. In fact, while the Kalundborg experiments were taking place in Denmark, a similar collaborative process called partnering evolved within the U.S. civil construction industry. The process by which partnering skills have grown from a limited experiment to an industry-wide competence looks much like the learning and investment process at OpWin.

Partnering in the U.S. Civil Construction Industry

Across the firms and government agencies that make up the U.S. civil construction industry, a collaborative process has emerged that has produced less carefully measured but quite probably larger percentage returns than those of the Kalundborg experiment. Moreover, the growing competence of U.S. firms in partnering has increased their ability to engage in new approaches to large construction projects, and partnering has become both a firm and an industry asset. In this sense, the collaborative skill of partnering has become a *meta-capability*.

While some collaborative problem solving among the various participants in large construction projects has always occurred, the process reached a new height in the late 1980s and early 1990s under the leadership of Colonel Charles E. Cowan, Director of the Portland District Office of the U.S. Army Corps of Engineers. Through several drafts of an ultimately widely used article, Cowan described the purpose and process of partnering.[6] Citing the growing cost of litigation and lack of creativity between construction project owners (various government agencies) and the construction firms that build their projects, he described a simple, trust-based process he and his staff were attempting to teach and follow in the U.S. Army Corps of Engineers.

One important component of this process was that the bid-winning construction firm, along with its major subcontractors, would be invited to a team-building workshop some weeks before the starting date of the project. At the workshop, key representatives from all parties—Army Corps project designers, construction firm managers, project superintendents, safety and value engineers, and subcontractor managers—would meet with skilled facilitators to build productive relationships, forge common understandings, and create trust among the parties.[7]

In 1989, the Portland Office launched a partnering experiment with a construction firm to build a large dam. To prepare for the team-building workshop, the project's resident Army Corps engineer and the construction firm's project manager attended a week-long leadership program that emphasized the team-building skills that the project would require. The subsequent three-day workshop involved key Army Corps personnel and their construction firm counterparts. Team-building consultants, who reinforced concepts the two top officials had covered in the leadership program, facilitated the workshop. This workshop produced several products, the most important of which was a charter that covered the project's goals, objectives, and expectations. The charter was signed by all of the workshop participants and displayed at the project's various locations.

The charter laid out guidelines for settling the inevitable issues that emerge with large construction projects. For example, design blueprints may need to be changed to accommodate unforeseen problems, and materials specifications may prove to be unattainable. Moreover, builder and/or owner engineers may discover creative ways to complete the project less expensively while improving its quality. Typically, the necessary steps to solve project problems and implement changes run into procedural and other types of barriers. Disputes may emerge, files are created to support possible legal claims, and delays and costs escalate.

This particular charter, however, set up procedures that assure that issues will be dealt with on the spot, within a short time period, or else sent to a higher level for timely resolution. The parties agreed to search for solutions by e-mail, telephone, or face-to-face meetings in order to avoid paper-based processes that always seem to lead to deeper and lengthier disputes.

As the dam project moved forward, members from both the Army Corps of Engineers and the construction firms sometimes found themselves falling back into traditional behavior patterns. The workshop leaders had prepared them for these occasions, and the charter was available to keep the dispute resolution process on track. Moreover, the partnering process not only provided procedures for dispute resolution, it also provided for review and learning sessions as the project progressed. A review halfway through the project made it clear that the charter goals of an early project finish, containment of unanticipated costs, and value-engineered design and process innovations estimated at $1 million or more were on their way to being achieved. The review validated the partnering process and reinforced the commitment of both the Army Corps and construction firm participants.

By 1992, Cowan had left the U.S. Army Corps of Engineers and become head of the Department of Transportation for the state of Arizona. He introduced the partnering process in Arizona, where it produced major gains, and the process then spread to some other states, most notably Texas and California. By 1996, Texas announced a second-generation partnering program, P2, which, in an agreement reached with the Associated General Contractors of Texas, made partnering a required element of every major construction project.

Today, the partnering process is observable, though unevenly, in civil construction projects throughout the United States. Skilled partnering firms are sought after as alliance partners by other construction firms, and the partnering process has helped to improve project quality and obtain cost savings at sufficient levels to maintain the industry's attention and use. Moreover, as more and more projects move toward what the industry refers to as the design-build approach, where coalitions of firms compete for the right to take the project from conception through completion, partnering skills become increasingly important to all of the parties involved. In these relationships, collaborative expertise can and does lead to innovation-driven value creation.

While contentious issues still abound in U.S. civil construction and, in many instances, lead to delays, increasing costs, and expensive legal wrangling, the partnering process is now firmly entrenched. It has been endorsed and institutionalized by the Associated General Contractors of America, and articles describing partnering successes and problems appear regularly in the industry's several commercial publications. The partnering process is now part of the curriculum in most professional seminars on engineering management and in many university construction engineering programs. Again, though limited to a single industry, the investments in collaborative capability being made by civil construction industry agencies, firms, and professional and educational institutions demonstrate the path toward the development of a value-creating meta-capability.

Acer Group's Business Federation Model

The partnering example in U.S. civil construction began as a conflict-resolution mechanism and gradually expanded into a means of solving a variety of problems encountered on construction projects as well as contributing to project innovations. However, neither the Danish industrial-municipal alliances nor the American partnering process represent full-blown examples of what we mean by collaboration as *joint enterprise*. Although both examples involve business situations, neither group of organizations is focused primarily on new products, services, or markets—and certainly not on *continuous* innovation.

The firm that we believe comes closest to practicing continuous innovation through collaboration on a large scale is the Acer Group. Based in Taiwan, Acer has thousands of employees, operations in forty-four countries, and dealer relationships in more than a hundred countries. With revenues of nearly $5 billion, Acer is the world's fifth-largest personal computer manufacturer, but it is in the process of transforming itself into a complete global information technology company that in recent years has started many successful e-business services.

Stan Shih, Acer's cofounder, chairman, and CEO, has designed Acer Group as a worldwide federation of companies held together by mutual interest and collaboration, not as a monolithic global corporation. Some units of Acer are wholly owned by the firm, while others (mainly marketing and distribution firms) are jointly owned by Acer and local investors. Both types of firms work willingly with the other companies in the federation because all firms have worked hard to become the preferred provider in their particular specialty or market. Acer helps its partner firms in other countries develop professional management, obtain investment funding, and become publicly owned because, according to Shih, "Owners take better care of their homes than renters." Acer's brand of collaborative capitalism is strongly entrenched in the global economy, particularly in emerging markets.

Acer has over forty separate business units grouped into four global business units. Several business units are R&D oriented, and these are based in Taiwan. Many of the remaining business units are marketing companies—advertising, selling, and servicing computers according to particular national or regional needs—and these units are spread around the world. Although each firm has a core task to perform, new product or service concepts can and do originate anywhere in the federation. Every new product proposal is evaluated as a business venture by the federation's partner firms because none of the firms is in a position to design, produce, and sell the product entirely by itself. Thus, at any given time, a number of collaborative efforts are underway throughout the federation, most of which involve innovation of some sort. The more recently developed Web-based service businesses originated mostly from the Taiwanese units and then spread around the federation as other units found local applications.

Interestingly, Shih has described Acer's philosophy of collaboration using the language and concepts of Go, an ancient Chinese board game. The objective in Go is to make parts of the game board inaccessible to your opponent and to acquire as much territory of your own as possible—clearly analogous to capturing market share in the business world. In Go, a good player follows the principle of *huo shih*, meaning to strengthen oneself by incorporating the strengths of others. Acer knows where the federation's strengths lie, and units work closely with each other to maximize the use of these strengths. Another principle found in Go is *wei kong*, meaning the encircling of unclaimed open territory, or approaching the core via the periphery. Acer has followed this principle in its international expansion, targeting collaborative efforts toward peripheral markets before tackling the bigger challenges of the U.S. and European markets. Lastly, a third principle is that of *huo yen*, meaning staying alive by linking independent units together. Acer has used this principle by creating largely independent business units that interact as a network of partners who trust each other and who respect each other's abilities.

Acer's approach, which is finding increasing favor among latecomer firms in both developed and developing economies, has elsewhere been called a *link-and-leverage strategy*.[8] Such a strategy contains the essential elements of our collaborative entrepreneurship model: a focus on innovation, a group of networked firms, and collaboration as the core operating capability. The major difference between Acer and OpWin, however, is that Acer's innovation process occurs up and down the value chain of the information technology industry whereas OpWin's innovative activities cut across industries.

Comparison of Actual Examples to OpWin Global Network

Two important observations can be made by comparing the real cases of Kalundborg, Denmark's industrial symbiosis, U.S. civil construction partnering, and Acer's business federation model with our fictional example of OpWin. First, collaboration can emerge spontaneously among various types of organizations if the necessary supporting conditions are present. Support begins with trusting relationships that allow information and know-how to be shared and applied to the process of wealth creation through innovation. Collaborating parties must engage in self-managing processes that are guided by trust and broad operating protocols rather than by hierarchical control. Moreover, where such processes exist, the participants appear to be as excited about the process of collaboration as they are about its results.

Second, the spontaneous revolution that energizes the collaborative process can be expanded and sustained if the participants understand the philosophy and methods of collaboration and if sufficient investments are made to grow trust and competence. The participants in the original OpWin alliance articulated a vision of an expanding network as well as the structure and process investments needed to make it work. The original firms, with the help of the Central Services Office, have guided and sustained growth both in the number of member firms and in the network's stock of collaborative capability. What all OpWin firms have learned is that if they behave in a competent and trustworthy manner, real economic gains can be consistently achieved—well beyond those achievable by the same firms acting alone.

Similarly, the initial collaborative projects at Kalundborg stimulated further voluntary projects in search of symbiotic linkage, but the spread of collaboration was also aided by a growing, shared vision of the process and its potential. Subsequent discussion enhanced understanding and promoted learning among both existing and new participants. In the construction partnering process, the initial vision was promoted by an articulate spokesperson, and subsequently, entire organizations supported and even championed the collaborative process and its results. Participants recognized that partnering would not simply occur but that it required an investment in time and training to build trust and learn collaborative procedures and processes. And at Acer, one can see how success creates its own momentum. Today, no unit within Acer's global federation of companies could imagine success coming from any approach other than its form of collaborative capitalism.

Conclusion

We believe that most collaboratively skilled organizations, even the pioneers described in this chapter, discover the power and versatility of collaboration only after they develop and use it for some limited purpose. Generally speaking, firms begin to collaborate with their suppliers and customers in order to improve their existing operations, such as reducing costs, increasing the speed of design and delivery, and enhancing flexibility all along the value chain. Organizations like OpWin, however, use their collaborative capability more broadly, such as finding creative ways to apply their know-how to both known and unknown markets. OpWin's member firms are part of a joint enterprise—they continually seek new products and new markets. Furthermore, the OpWin network is a mechanism that non-member firms may join temporarily in order to pursue their own commercial ideas and goals. Thus, OpWin has both actual and potential wealth-generating value.

We also believe that in the future collaborative capability is more likely to diffuse among organizations only after appropriate investments are made. The reason that collaboration, particularly among supply chain partners, is usually fragmented and short-lived is because all of the investments needed to grow and sustain it are seldom made. For the most part, those investments and risk-taking approaches are not legitimated by today's widely held beliefs about how organizations work and how they should be managed. In the next chapter, we will discuss the main barriers that stand in the way of the development of collaboration-driven innovation.

We showed a draft of the preceding chapters to a former CEO, a talented and accomplished business executive, and asked for his reaction. He later told one of us:

> This sounds good, but it won't work. First of all, you're going to have to write another book that explains exactly how you can put this thing together legally. Secondly, it's way too complex. How can anyone manage an organization like this? In my experience, putting together even a temporary alliance among two or three firms requires an enormous amount of effort and usually doesn't generate much in the way of results. Given the hassle of managing an alliance, as well as the likelihood that one of the parties will try to take advantage of you, I think you're better off going it alone. When you keep innovation inside your own firm, you can control the process. You can prevent information leaks and make certain that any returns go straight to your own bottom line rather than filling the pockets of managers in another company. Even if, as you claim, firms may waste as much as 80 percent of their potential to innovate, I still say a firm should go it alone. In fact, I'd rather see the 80 percent go to waste than to run the risk that someone else will take advantage of me or my firm.

This executive's statements about OpWin reflect what he has been taught both in business school and in his climb up the corporate ladder of several business firms. Moreover, the institutions that support and regulate the modern business enterprise reinforce his views. Given this context, any group of firms that attempted to organize like OpWin would face an uphill battle as they struggled to become a viable organization.

Altogether, we can identify five categories of barriers that OpWin-like firms face: organizational, institutional, societal, philosophical, and conceptual. In this chapter, we will describe each type of barrier and show how it retards the development of a multi-firm collaborative network organization. On the one hand, the organizational, institutional, and societal barriers probably will be obvious to anyone familiar with organizations and how they work. On the other hand, the philosophical and conceptual barriers are not only less obvious but also much more difficult to overcome. In pointing out the various barriers to the development of a multi-firm collaborative network, we do not intend to stifle interest in this powerful new form of organizing. Rather, we believe that identifying these barriers is the first step in overcoming them.

Organizational Barriers

Most organization structures create and sustain tight departmentalization of some kind. Whether organizational units are focused on market segments (divisions), specialized expertise (functions), or even a particular point along the industry value chain (supplier, manufacturer, distributor, etc.), boundaries emerge that are often difficult to penetrate and which may make intra- and inter-firm collaboration unlikely to occur smoothly if at all. How information flows, performance is evaluated, and rewards are allocated are heavily influenced by unit boundaries, and those boundaries reinforce we-versus-they thinking in regard to potential knowledge development and innovation.

Generally speaking, the biggest organizational barrier to operating tomorrow's innovative firms is everything that managers have learned about how to operate today's organizations. Leadership and planning approaches, control and reward systems, decision-making processes—each of these organizational mechanisms will have to be rethought to fit the new business and organizational models represented by OpWin.

Institutional Barriers

Similarly, the various laws and practices that have been developed so that business can be conducted in a fair and orderly manner are also based on traditional types of organizations. Therefore, today's institutional environment is not particularly conducive to the construction or management of a new type of organization like OpWin. For example, current accounting conventions represent a barrier to continuous innovation as practiced at OpWin. The time, training, and money required to build collaborative capability within and across firms are crucial investments to the success of OpWin. Under current accounting rules, however, such investments must be carried on a firm's books as general and administrative expenses, and G&A is always subject to tight control and is a continuing target for cost reduction in order to increase current profitability.

The trust necessary to collaborate also depends on investments of time and money in trust-building activities, including staff training and the development of knowledge-management systems (internal and external to the organization). Organization members learn to trust those above them, and those in other departments and partner firms, through working together on projects, the opportunity to ask questions and consider responses, and so forth. Again, the expenditures essential to construct and operate those activities most likely will end up being classified as G&A.

A particularly troublesome institutional barrier is the problem of valuing and accounting for intellectual capital. In a knowledge-intensive organization such as OpWin, only a fraction of the total market value is represented by tangible assets such as capital equipment, inventories, or real estate. The bulk of OpWin's market value rests on the belief that OpWin has the know-how and the ability to sustain and grow a revenue stream largely dependent on products and services it has not yet created. That know-how is held in the heads of individuals in OpWin's member and affiliate firms, and it is voluntarily offered and used. However, because it is voluntary, it can also be withheld, and it can leave the firm usually without recourse. The expenditures essential to holding, growing, and encouraging the sharing of knowledge assets are treated not as investments but rather as expenses constantly subject to review and reduction. More than thirty years ago, Rensis E. Likert suggested that firms should develop a means of accounting for their human assets, giving them status equal to that of a capital investment. His suggestion is only just now beginning to show practical utility under the banner of *knowledge management*.[1]

Societal Barriers

In a business world dominated by traditional organizations and supported by a well-established institutional environment, the meta-capability of inter-firm collaboration needed to energize and operate an OpWin-like organization is likely to develop slowly and unevenly. Some firms, and perhaps even entire nations, might accelerate the evolutionary process by investing money, time, experimentation, and other resources in an effort to develop the new meta-capability ahead of their competitors. However, in order for collaboration to become a widely dispersed societal asset, it will require an enormous amount of childhood education and training, large and continuing investments of various kinds by firms, and collective will on the part of individuals, firms, and governmental bodies.

It will also require changes in how we keep track of a nation's progress. Traditional economic measures such as gross domestic product, productivity, corporate profits, and personal savings are valid indicators of overall economic development, but they reveal little about the current or future wealth generated from innovation. Such measures also do not reflect the level of investments being made to develop the knowledge and learning skills needed for future collaboration and innovation. Measures of human capital that can be used to identify the level of current capabilities and to serve as benchmarks for evaluating the impact of future investments are being explored by a few European countries, but such social indicators require much more development if collaboration is to become a true meta-capability.[2]

Philosophical Barriers

Some less obvious barriers also stand in OpWin's way. For example, economic explanations concerning how wealth is created and allocated, and the legal concept of ownership rights, result from the emphasis in Western societies (especially the United States) on social philosophies that assert the virtues of self-determination and self-reliance. The general justification for free markets as the mechanism for generating and distributing wealth, and the related justification for the ownership and control of that wealth, has roots in the philosophy of liberal individualism, which maintains that society is best served by individuals who freely pursue their own destinies.

Countering beliefs that private ownership and self-determination produce the optimal development and allocation of societal assets, collectivist or socialistic philosophies argue for common (state) ownership of key means of production and the allocation of wealth based on need as well as contribution. Socialist philosophies reflect the fundamental belief that private ownership perpetuates inequities and that market allocation of resources is rife with imperfections and exploitation. Most modern Western societies have blended libertarian and socialist philosophies by developing sociopolitical and economic systems that couple private ownership and market mechanisms with state ownership and control of infrastructure mechanisms (such as public education). In addition, Western societies provide safety net programs to ameliorate the plight of marginalized members of society.

However, both the dominant belief in the virtues of free markets and self-determination, and the beliefs in the need for state ownership and investment in human capital, focus attention primarily on the distribution of societal wealth, not on its generation. Moreover, neither philosophy provides foundational values for the development of the collaborative competence required for an OpWin-like strategy and structure. That is, common ownership of key resources, and the commitment of resources to joint innovative activity without prior agreement on the precise terms of returns allocation, is either counter to or outside the reach of current social philosophies.

Over the last few years, the primacy of ownership and asset-allocation issues in both the individualistic and collectivistic philosophies has created increasing scrutiny of opportunistic behavior. Concern over the diversion of owner (financial investor) assets by self-serving agents (managers) is reflected in the current heated debate about corporate governance.[3] Clearly, when the conversation of management is primarily about how to protect against both internal and external opportunism, it is difficult for managers to consider arguments for trust building or for making substantial investments in the development of collaborative capability.

Conceptual Barriers

In addition to the fact that Western social philosophies do not directly encourage the development of collaborative entrepreneurship, there are conceptual barriers to the construction of multi-firm organizations like OpWin. For example, it is clear from our executive friend's statement that he is judging OpWin according to his personal conception of a business firm. Viewed from the perspective of a tightly managed, hierarchical company—the kind of firm he has typically led or worked for—OpWin appears to be overly complex and all but impossible to construct and operate. And, if seen from that perspective, it certainly is.

Indeed, the primary reason that OpWin does not yet exist is that only a few people are even thinking about this type of organization—and those who are cannot fully describe how it operates or prove that it will work. If one cannot conceive of or justify something, then it is quite unlikely that it will become a reality. Although OpWin contains familiar components, such as firms and alliances, its overall package of resources is new. OpWin requires managers to imagine an organization composed of many independent firms, a business model of nonstop product and service innovation, the open sharing of information across firms to foster collaboration, and a governance system of self-management instead of hierarchical direction and control. This new combination of resources is not easy to comprehend when one's experience comes entirely from traditional types of organizations.

Furthermore, the executive's comments on OpWin reflect his formal education and subsequent learning experiences. He has studied economic and business theories that explain and justify the roles of markets, firms, and management processes in the U.S. economic system, and he is well versed in the conventional wisdom promulgated by the business press and management consultants. Although pioneering entrepreneurs and managers drive change in organizational practice, economic and business theory eventually catch up to explain the underlying forces shaping business decision-making and behavior. In doing so, theory helps not only to spread the new practice, but it also serves as justification for other managers to follow and as rationalization for the changes that need to be made in the institutional realm to facilitate the new practice. Thus, to a considerable extent, the theorist's *de*scriptions become the manager's *pre*scriptions.

Reflecting this continuing cycle from practice to theory and back to practice, business and economic theory, since the time of the Industrial Revolution, has evolved to explain the increasing diversity and complexity of both firms and markets. However, while current theory can provide explanations and support for the development of large, diversified business enterprises operating in a global economy, it cannot yet easily accommodate a network of independent firms engaging in collaborative entrepreneurship. In the following paragraphs, we will briefly describe how these theories have evolved, following a path that appears to be moving in a direction that could at some point include an OpWin-like organizational form. At the same time, however, the continuing heavy theoretical emphasis on the appropriation and allocation of economic wealth clearly does not support investments in the collaborative capability needed by futuristic organizations like OpWin. Our brief historical tour of the theory of the firm will point out where the theory is today and the refocusing that needs to occur for the theory to truly support and justify the next generation of organizations.

The initial theory of the firm

Early economic descriptions of the business enterprise and managerial behavior started with the notion of production not of a firm. A firm was simply a group of individuals who came together to transform inputs into outputs (a single product or a limited range of products). The necessary inputs to production were secured in the spot (short-term) market, and the main decision-making variables were the determination of optimal production levels and the appropriate mix of the different types of inputs. This theory of production operated under the assumption that all firms had complete information and that there was a perfectly competitive market and therefore no economic profit (only a normal return to each of the factors of production such as labor, capital, etc.). In this conception of the firm and its markets, there was virtually no need for the firm to develop what we refer to today as a competitive strategy.

With the advent of the modern industrial era and the emergence of a few very large firms, economic theory faced two major challenges. The first challenge was to explain why large firms arose, firms that disobeyed the laws of perfect competition by hiring permanent employees, making investments in assets for their exclusive use over the long run rather than using spot-market transactions, and operating on a scale larger than their competitors thereby lowering input costs. Economic theory eventually developed to the point where it could explain transactions that occurred inside large firms rather than in the market.[4]

The second challenge to the initial theory of the firm was the fact that some firms began to earn above-normal profits (so-called economic rents). Such firms could set prices themselves rather than have them set by the market and could lead the industry in other ways rather than simply react to market forces. A new branch of economics, which came to be called industrial organization economics, studied the phenomenon of the abnormally large firm and described how it developed scale economies, erected barriers to entry into the industry, and exerted power relative to its competitors. Thus, in a growing number of industries, perfect competition gave way to oligopoly where a handful of firms could appropriate extraordinary returns.[5]

Such modifications and extensions of theory not only provided an explanation for what was happening in business; they also helped to justify and promote the observed behavior. For example, managers who wished to expand their firms could go to the capital markets and argue for the pursuit of scale economies, better control over transaction costs, and increased market predictability as rationale for the needed investment capital. Similarly, governmental and other institutional bodies now had a theory-based logic for altering their approaches (e.g., to antitrust law or industrial regulation), and business professors and consultants could study the structure and management of large firms and teach those approaches to students and executives.

From single business to multi-business firms

Over time, some large firms began to bump up against the limits of operating in a single industry or industry segment. For example, market size hindered their continued expansion and profitability, or regulatory bodies started to worry about their increasingly monopolistic power. Consequently, those firms began to move into additional markets where they could more fully utilize the resources they had access to or controlled. Once again, the success of such pioneering firms in appropriating excess profits challenged existing economic theory and its assumptions.

In response, the theory of the firm began to shift its focus from economies of scale to economies of scope. The returns of diversification (scope) were compared with those of single-business firms, and the data showed that firms that diversified into related products and markets had superior performance.[6] Business scholars studied the internal processes of multi-business firms and showed how they could achieve synergies across their businesses, leverage their brands and other resources (especially organizational and managerial knowhow) to enter new markets, and mitigate the risks of doing business in one or only a few industries.

As before, the theoretical explanations provided impetus to changes in business practice. Investment in diversification now had a scientific rationale, and consultants scrambled to develop portfolio approaches that helped managers to understand and develop an optimal mix of businesses for their firms.[7] In boardrooms and classrooms across the United States, executives and future executives learned about the power of the related diversifier firm. Indeed, in the 1960s, the U.S. model of the diversified multinational corporation began to be emulated by firms around the world, first in Europe and later in Japan.[8]

From tangible to intangible assets

During the last decade or so, economic and management research has focused on explaining why some firms appear to be able to earn excess profits because of their know-how and capability. That is, even among firms that are similarly organized and apparently pursuing similar strategies, some seem to have management expertise that allows them to do things better and/or quicker than their competitors. This theoretical focus has given rise to the resource-based view of the firm.[9] Moreover, according to this view, it is not the mere possession of resources that leads to competitive advantages; it is the uncommon ability to use those resources that is crucial. This rudimentary theory recognizes that resources are not spread evenly across firms in an industry, and more importantly, that putting resources together and applying them creatively goes well beyond the optimization of known production functions. Some firms are, in fact, more capable than others, and they are able to leverage their knowledge and abilities to appropriate an inordinate slice of an industry's profits.

Interestingly, this general observation has led many firms in recent years to narrow their scope and to focus on particular aspects of the industry value chain where their core competencies can lead to a competitive advantage.[10] Such value chain reconfiguration is reflected in the rise of strategic alliances and the current interest in supply chain management. The overall idea is that firms can achieve abnormal profits by performing only certain value-adding functions and then contracting with other firms to complete the business offering. In theoretical language, the resource-based perspective is evolving into the dynamic capabilities perspective in which a firm is expected to continually develop its package of resources and skills so that the firm can both meet and lead industry change.[11]

As in previous eras, the iterative interaction of research and practice is presently shifting the scholarly and practical focus to resources and capabilities as the source of firm profitability. Books and seminars on how to develop and apply capabilities are now an integral part of business education. Consultants and the business press, as well as the capital markets, encourage firms to focus on those areas where they can add value and to work with other firms to maximize value both up and down their particular value chain. There is an accompanying interest in organizational learning and knowledge management as methods for deepening and extending firm capabilities, reflected in the rise of executive roles such as Chief Knowledge Officer and Chief Learning Officer.[12] On the institutional front, regulations regarding interactions among firms have relaxed somewhat so that companies can now work more closely together to develop and use their joint capabilities.

The current theory of the firm

More than eighty years have passed since economists first defined the purpose and operation of the modern business firm. We believe that economic and management theory has made three main advances during this period. First, current theory focuses on the kinds of firms that actually exist—as opposed to the initial characterization of a small one-product company competing against dozens of other small companies of exactly the same size and using exactly the same methods. Now, in addition to the many small firms that dot the competitive landscape, we routinely refer to large, diversified corporations, and we know a lot about how they operate within and across industries and countries. On the other hand, the network form of organizing, whereby groups of firms link themselves together in order to compete more effectively, is a relatively recent arrival to the organizational literature. Therefore, although multi-firm supply chain networks are recognized by theory, they are only just beginning to be thoroughly studied empirically.

Second, theory more accurately accounts for how firms compete. Most industries are neither monopolistic nor perfectly competitive but rather reflect some form of oligopolistic competition. In an oligopoly, several firms dominate the industry. They exert power and leadership, and smaller, less influential firms in the industry must learn how to live within the shadow of the major players. The literature contains a wealth of strategies that both large and small firms can use to survive and flourish in this type of competitive environment.[13] Furthermore, the literature is beginning to reflect firms' increasing use of co-opetition (simultaneous cooperation and competition) and to describe how firms behave when they engage in multi-market competition. Despite these advances, however, the literature on how firms can compete through collaboration is just now beginning to develop.[14]

Third, theorists generally agree that how firms are managed matters. That is, a firm's fate is largely a result of how it conducts itself—the capabilities it develops, how it assembles and uses resources, and so on.[15] In addition, most theorists now view the firm as a dynamic entity, one that can learn about and adapt to its environment over time.[16]

In summary, the growing theoretical focus on wealth creation through the accumulation of unique resources, particularly managerial know-how and other learned capabilities, is supportive of continuing investments in human and social capital. However, such investments are still typically envisioned as being made within and owned exclusively by a single firm.

Redirecting the theory of the firm

As we have argued, the evolving theory of the firm, as developed by scholars in economics and management, has had a decided influence on business practice. Unfortunately, however, current theory always reflects *past* practice. Therefore, in those firms that wish to pursue the new strategy of continuous innovation, managers' efforts to build the needed multi-firm network organization are simply not supported or legitimated by the theory in its present form. How then can the theory of the firm be redirected in order to make it more useful?

One major shortcoming of the theory of the firm, as previously suggested, is that it focuses on the behavior of a single firm rather than *groups of firms*. Managers who wish to pursue a strategy of continuous innovation à la OpWin will rely on resources and capabilities jointly owned by multiple firms. The theory of the firm needs to expand its unit of analysis to incorporate joint ownership of assets and resources. Given that the current concept of the firm is that of a mechanism for accumulating and employing commonly held resources, extending this view to include networks of independent firms sharing a common resource would seem to us to be a logical extension. In a trust-supported organization of independent firms, one could expect knowledge resources to be exchanged with low costs and high returns.

Another shortcoming concerns the role of *capabilities* in a multi-firm network. The current theory of the firm, as reflected in the resource-based view and the dynamic capabilities perspective, portrays firms as using their capabilities to identify, assemble, and use resources to achieve profitability and sustainable competitive advantages. However, the theory does not specify how to measure capabilities or how to evaluate their contribution to firm performance. This theoretical deficiency is especially apparent in reference to intangible assets. For example, the capabilities needed to efficiently use physical assets, such as money, land, buildings, and equipment, are well known and widely understood by managers. On the other hand, it is much more difficult to determine the skills that are needed to develop relational capital between two or more firms or how much such capability contributes to a firm's performance. Once we have determined how to define and account for capabilities, we can begin to reward those managers who help their firms become more capable.

A third shortcoming of current theory is that it lacks concepts and methods to measure *wealth creation* and the *investments* required to generate wealth. The various member firms of OpWin collaborate with each other to pursue product and market innovations without a prior concern for the distribution of returns. However, those firms have no way of justifying their behavior economically. Although they are clearly investing time and other resources in collaborative activities, they cannot calculate the returns on those investments in terms of the wealth that they create using traditional tools and approaches.[17]

A final—and clearly the most fundamental—shortcoming of the theory of the firm is its flawed conception of human motivation. The theory assumes that people in organizations act only in their own self-interest and often with guile, and the entire theoretical apparatus is built on this faulty assumption. Other human motives, such as sharing, working together, or being generous, have no place in the current theory of the firm and, by implication, are illegitimate behaviors in organizations. And yet such motives and behaviors are critical to the success of an organization like OpWin. In business schools, economics departments, executive training programs, and wherever else the theory of the firm is being taught, it needs to be expanded to include the positive motives of human beings and the implications of those motives for business decision making and management.[18]

Conclusion

Although the creation of an OpWin-like organization faces many imposing barriers, most of the conceptual, legal, and institutional constraints that have been erected in support of current strategy, structure, capability, and process packages can and will be removed as collaborative entrepreneurship proves its merits as a wealth-creating process. Societal and philosophical barriers will also change, but only slowly as younger generations of people are taught and embrace the new values. Of course, it would be helpful to OpWin-like firms if societal investments in human assets enjoyed greater support, and if exploitative behavior on the part of individuals and firms were more widely condemned, but OpWin-like experiments can nevertheless succeed if their designers are fully committed. Indeed, as businesspeople have repeatedly demonstrated, there is not only a large potential gain but great satisfaction in "doing things differently." In fact, this is a basic motivation common to most entrepreneurs.

8   Getting Past the Barriers

While the barriers discussed in the previous chapter are indeed formidable, past experience suggests that some of them would fall rather quickly for those firms that make a concerted push toward a new organizational form such as that of collaborative entrepreneurship. Indeed, the overall purpose of a new organizational form is to remove existing barriers to the pursuit of new strategies. Moreover, institutional norms, rules, and procedures change over time to accommodate successful new strategies and structures. The required social and human capital investments will eventually be made, but in the short run firms committed to new approaches can create new skills, attitudes, and values through their own well-conceived investments. They can become, in effect, the lead investors in developing societal assets.

Ideological and conceptual barriers, however, are far more troublesome because they block out even the consideration of new strategic and organizational approaches. Rational arguments in support of new ways to organize are hard to mount in the face of strongly held attitudes and beliefs. Given the sizable ideological barriers we have described, the reader understandably may wonder, how close is OpWin to becoming a reality? We would like to address this question by first providing a brief summary and justification of our core arguments and then by describing the key actions that firms must take in order for the concept of collaborative entrepreneurship to take hold and grow.

The Case for OpWin

Our main premise has been that twenty-first century firms in advanced economies will compete increasingly at the downstream end of industry value chains, utilizing their superior knowledge-creating capability to generate a continuous and growing stream of innovative products and services. However, most firms are enjoying only limited success in exploiting their know-how because (a) existing organizational structures and processes impede internal knowledge flows, and (b) restrictive market strategies constrain those innovations that do manage to surface.

Entrepreneurs, as we have described, solve these problems by reshaping underdeveloped ideas and recombining resource packages that bring those ideas into contact with new market opportunities. However, entrepreneurs experience high failure rates. The entrepreneurial process is both disruptive and valuable, but it has neither the efficiency nor the continuity to make it an attractive long-term corporate strategy.

Thus, our argument continues, the challenge is to create a new organizational form—a new market strategy less impeded by existing firm and industry boundaries, and a new structure less hierarchically constrained and with managerial processes that allow ideas and resources to be shared, reshaped, and exploited. Such a form, ideally, would be both entrepreneurial *and* efficient.

The OpWin model of collaborative entrepreneurship, we conclude, is a logical extension of this line of reasoning. The model features a collaborative network of firms rather than a single entity in order to maximize the opportunity of ideas to realize their economic value through exploration across myriad complementary markets. It is designed as a partnership among independent firms that maximizes the freedom of individual units to manage and benefit from collaborative innovation that they themselves have initiated. It is managed laterally rather than vertically to minimize hierarchical constraints on the generation and sharing of ideas. It utilizes the funds that would ordinarily be spent to centrally protect intellectual property to build, instead, trusting relationships and protocols to facilitate multilateral sharing and innovation. And, lastly, the model's management processes—particularly its reward system—are designed to focus the attention of all of its member firms on the creation of economic value rather than its appropriation.

However, to many people, the OpWin model is so conceptually and ideologically jarring that its underlying logic is obscured. For those people, it is difficult to even set the agenda for a productive debate. Nevertheless, we see two approaches that might allow us to move forward in terms of helping managers start a conversation about the merits of an OpWin-like organization.

One approach begins by listing the crucial features of the ideal modern firm and then examining how well the OpWin form mirrors those characteristics. For example, among the most commonly heard adjectives or phrases that describe the ideal firm are "market driven," "flexible," "customer oriented," "cost efficient," "high performing," and "sustainable." How well does OpWin stack up against these criteria?

An alternative approach identifies and responds to the major concerns that the OpWin model elicits among managers, investors, customers, and other relevant stakeholders. Indeed, one might extend the stakeholder list to include management theorists and writers as well as economists. For example, managers might be most concerned that their individual progress and rewards are overlooked in the complexity of a collaborative multi-firm network. Investors might be worried that a given firm in which they hold stock would obtain lower returns from a collaborative project than it could from the individual pursuit of its innovative idea. Customers might raise issues concerning guarantees and/or liabilities related to products or services that are jointly designed and produced. Lastly, management writers might be concerned that the new form is not sustainable, and management theorists and economists might favor other ways to increase innovation capacity.

Let us examine OpWin with respect to each of these evaluative approaches.

OpWin and the Ideal Firm

At first glance, traditionally trained managers may see OpWin as the antithesis of the ideal modern firm. After all, it celebrates collaborative achievement and demands a primary focus on joint equity over individual rewards. Upon closer examination, however, we believe that OpWin compares favorably on the list of ideal criteria. For example, the OpWin model has the potential to be the ultimate market-driven firm, primarily because it is designed to be responsive to signals from not one but many markets. Ideas that would be tossed aside because they do not fit a firm's primary market may have high value when modified to meet customer needs in another market. Indeed, the major purpose of OpWin is to minimize the constraints that current market foci place on the utilization of a firm's know-how.

Similarly, the emphasis on collaboration may imply to many that OpWin is not prepared for tough competition or has little concern for cost effectiveness. Again, a close examination suggests that while inter-firm teams may collaborate on the design of innovative products and services, team success at OpWin is measured by the same criterion of customer acceptance faced by more traditional firms. Of course, OpWin's innovative designs do fail from time to time, just as do those of its competitors. The difference is that member firms in the OpWin network have a much deeper reservoir of know-how than their competitors of similar and even larger size.

Lastly, OpWin faces the same challenges of sustainability and growth in the face of constantly changing technologies and markets faced by other firms, but it has the capability to both export its existing know-how to new arenas and to import knowledge relevant to its existing markets. OpWin firms are not only less market-bound than their peers, their trade channels are flexible rather than fixed. At any point in time, an OpWin firm's ability to rearrange its resources and realign them with other markets is vastly superior to that of traditionally organized firms. Indeed, the OpWin firm can be as entrepreneurial—as constantly renewable—as its growing capability to collaborate allows.

Stakeholder concerns about OpWin

A major complaint among managers in traditional organizations is that their innovative ideas are either ignored or stolen by their peers or superiors. Knowledge transfer in such settings obviously suffers as managers seek to get their ideas heard while protecting their ownership. For managers conditioned by this type of environment, OpWin may appear to provide even less opportunity for them to protect their ideas and obtain appropriate credit for their contributions. After all, in OpWin, it is anticipated that many ideas emerging in one firm may flower months later in another firm elsewhere in the network.

Such managerial concerns have merit—ideas do indeed flow freely across firm and national borders in OpWin Global Network. However, they do so only because OpWin's system is designed and dedicated to allay its members' concerns and ensure equitable recognition and rewards. Organization members do not have to worry about the loss of their intellectual property or depend on their superiors to recognize the value of their ideas and provide the personal recognition they are due. Equity is everyone's responsibility. It is a responsibility that is explicit and continuously upheld in all of OpWin's procedures, so much so that it is confidently put out of mind during the process of idea sharing.

OpWin firms understand that opportunistic behavior is learned and reinforced by traditional control and reward systems. By making equitable recognition everyone's responsibility, and by investing in orientation, training, and protocol development to assist members in pursuing equity, OpWin seeks to refocus competitive energy away from its internal operations and toward market opportunities where it can exploit its innovation-driven first-mover advantage.

Investors, as stakeholders, may not be particularly impressed that OpWin is dedicated to ensuring internal equity by making recognition everyone's responsibility and by investing in orientation, training, and protocol development. Rather, investors are primarily focused on growing and protecting a large and sustainable earnings stream. Indeed, investors in individual OpWin firms may be most concerned that another OpWin firm, in which they have no equity stake, is the prime beneficiary of an idea that originated in "their" firm.

However, OpWin would counter that every firm in its network is more, rather than less, likely to collect a rightful share of the returns from its intellectual property precisely because OpWin has minimized the likelihood that internal opportunism will occur. In OpWin, ideas are openly shared through voluntary bilateral agreement, supported not just by legal protection but also by the full force of a community commitment to equity. The members of an OpWin-like network recognize that their community membership, with its shared knowledge base and broad market linkages, is their most important asset—an asset not to be risked by even the appearance of opportunistic behavior.

Similarly, customers could be assumed to bear greater risk from products and services jointly designed, produced, and distributed by two or more OpWin network members. Where, it might be asked, does responsibility for customer satisfaction and well-being fall? Such customer concerns, of course, are not unique to an OpWin-like organization. Design, distribution, and service are regularly divided among several firms along the value chain, and it is not uncommon for firms in traditional value chains to attempt to push customer suggestions or complaints upstream to producers and suppliers.

OpWin's commitment to equity across all stakeholders enhances customer service and satisfaction. Network partners who have learned to treat one another with caring trust are likely to share that commitment in all of their interactions. Thus, commitment to customer satisfaction is not just a marketing issue with OpWin firms; it is a part of their community code.

The Key Challenge for Firms: Designing Collaborative Reward and Control Systems

Multi-firm collaborative networks, we believe, will be built one firm at a time around a small core group of firms that have a shared vision, a common set of values, competence in collaboration, and a conveniently accessible and usable knowledge base. Such networks will grow and become more successful as a result of their large and continuing investments in human and knowledge capital. Collaborative competency must be developed among individuals, teams, and firms, and trust must become a systemwide asset.

Firms that are interested in pursuing a continuous innovation strategy need to invest heavily in reward and control systems that support collaboration, as opposed to current systems that favor competition and cooperation. Redesigning control systems will be less challenging than redesigning reward systems. Most managers already know how to decentralize responsibility for control to departments and even to the level of the workgroup or team. Certainly, modern communications and decision-making technologies have aided in this process (though they also have provided a seductive opportunity for higher-level managers to second-guess and intervene). True collaboration, however, requires widespread self-control.

Fortunately, the newer management skill of protocol building can be used to guide the design of department, team, and individual control systems that have little need for hierarchical intervention. Recall from our discussion of protocols in the construction partnering process that a key outcome was a series of agreements about when and how decisions would be made and disputes resolved. Firms that seek to build and support collaborative capability will benefit from creating such operating protocols. Thoughtfully designed protocols can support any type of delegation process and can improve local control by giving both organizational units and teams the assurance that they will not be subject to hierarchical intervention. Such protocols not only support self-governance, they also assure higher management that decisions will be made quickly at lower levels or else voluntarily brought to their attention.

Individuals, teams, and firms in a multi-firm collaborative network need the assurance of predictable behaviors and common expectations. Well-understood and practiced protocols for forming collaborative relationships, and for developing and introducing product or market innovations, can substitute for the lengthy process of trust building required by traditional control systems. Protocols allow for self-control among teams and firms, and if honored faithfully, they almost guarantee that the environment essential to collaborative effort will be maintained.[1]

Turning to reward systems, it is increasingly well understood that innovation is based on the collaborative creation and sharing of knowledge, both explicit and tacit, and that such sharing is primarily intrinsically motivated. Indeed, as we illustrated earlier, efforts to hierarchically direct and monetarily reward knowledge sharing are usually counterproductive.[2] People share knowledge because the process is exciting and rewarding in and of itself. Once incentives are introduced, participants are likely to begin to calculate the value of their contributions, and the voluntary sharing of knowledge is diminished.

Presently, it appears that we know more about what not to do than about what to do in terms of designing reward systems that support collaborative entrepreneurship. The guiding principle in reward-system design for innovation is to structure rewards so that they do not intrude on the innovation process. At OpWin, the cornerstones of its reward system are competitive salaries and benefits coupled with the likelihood of long-term returns from collaboration. That reward system removes much of the concern for current needs and promotes long-term security. Moreover, it offers the strong possibility of future wealth without forcing that goal on the immediate process of collaborative sharing. OpWin's protocol that idea users must reward idea providers in a mutually satisfactory way pushes the calculation of returns to the background and keeps the spotlight on innovation.

Similarly, OpWin's focus on meeting the needs of all of its stakeholders—customers, member and affiliate firms, local communities, and the natural environment—provides OpWin members the pride of belonging to an organization that "does the right thing" and is therefore deserving of respect. Historically, corporations have been chartered to achieve not only an economic purpose but also to advance the public good. Thus, the widely held belief, particularly among American managers, that a corporation exists for the sole benefit of its shareholders is both legally wrong (shareholders only have a claim on a firm's future revenue streams) and morally deficient (firms should promote the public good not just shareholder interests). OpWin's demonstrated intent to do the right thing is entirely consistent with the expected role of an economic entity. And in

OpWin, opportunistic behavior is seen as aberrant, not as the norm. Feeling good about one's organization and what it is accomplishing for society is thus an important part of the intrinsic motivation that underlies OpWin's reward system.

In summary, we imagine that emerging multi-firm collaborative networks will be designed primarily for self-control and intrinsic motivation. Designers will need to identify and link up with firms whose managers hold similar attitudes. Our belief is that, overall, collaborative networks will evolve reward and control systems that are as creative (and as collaboratively designed) as their products and services.

Conclusion

We have implied throughout this book that OpWin could serve as a recipe for the creation of similar collaborative networks among existing firms. Of course, the precise mix of ingredients, and the process by which they are assembled and developed, will vary according to the unique circumstances facing the founding firms and their industry challenges and opportunities. What cannot vary, however, if the new resource package is to succeed, is the requirement that all of the needed elements are included and that conflicting elements are removed.

For a real OpWin to succeed, the new resource package and its supporting rationale must be fully understood by network members, and investments must be made to develop appropriate capabilities. Equally important, existing organizational features, especially those associated with controls and rewards, must be carefully analyzed and, in many cases, largely dismantled. Even though new control and reward systems are put in place to support collaborative entrepreneurship, remnants of the old system may still attract attention and present barriers to the development of trust-based intrinsic motivation. Psychologically, the gestalt of collaboration needs to be internalized by everyone.

As has been the case before, we anticipate that those firms that achieve the most complete redesign will not only enjoy the largest success but will make the new approach appear to be natural and easy to operate. Those multi-firm network pioneers will then point the way for other firms to follow.

How long will all of this take? We predict that OpWin will become a reality within the next ten years. Managers already know how to build and operate international multi-firm network organizations. If our and other industrial societies will invest in the development and diffusion of collaborative capability, then OpWin's package will be complete.

9 Conclusion

During the telecast of the National Football League's Super Bowl on February 1, 2004, IBM sponsored an advertisement during halftime that featured Muhammad Ali encouraging a small boy to bravely and boldly realize his potential. The ad closed with an image of two words placed one over the other:

IBM

Linux

The idea that the world's most prolific generator of patents— the heavyweight champion of information technology, if you will— would so publicly tie its future potential to an open software design dependent on collaborative innovation was eye-opening. There are, of course, many strategic reasons for IBM's use of the Linux system. Nevertheless, in our view, this dramatic public linkage clearly indicates that the leading edge of business is moving in a direction supportive of collaborative entrepreneurship.

Indeed, IBM's ad can be viewed as the symbolic centerpiece of a constantly enlarging set of articles, books, Web sites, and symposia exploring the collaborative process and its potential for business enterprise. Moreover, in our opinion, the pace at which attention is being focused on collaboration is quickening. The next economic upswing will very likely feature information technology, biotechnology, and nanotechnology industries—arenas in which collaboration among business firms, venture capitalists, universities, and public institutions has a high potential payoff. Firms in these industries, which span traditional industry demarcations, may find it valuable—perhaps even imperative—to move faster in the direction of collaborative entrepreneurship than even our optimistic forecasts suggest.

Moreover, the alternative approach to competitive success, the creation of economic value through cost cutting and process improvements, is fast becoming unattractive. Although there were major productivity gains made in the 1990s, there is now wide agreement that continuous efforts to reduce labor costs, including layoffs associated with outsourcing, have decreased employee morale and loyalty. Moreover, reduced service and increased fees, along with harassing sales efforts and the exploitation of customer information, have generally damaged public confidence and trust in business firms and their managers.[1]

The next stage of capitalism, we are convinced, will exploit the wealth-creating power of continuous innovation. But first firms must rebuild trust. They must divert the dollars now being poured into the marginal gains that can be expected in process efficiencies into efforts to rebuild employee and customer trust and loyalty. Then they must invest that trust capital in the development of collaboration, with the objective of creating a meta-capability upon which future business can be based.

This book has focused on approaches to trust building and collaborative capability within our hypothetical OpWin Global Network and among real firms and agencies in various industries and economies. We have attempted to build the case that trust and collaborative skills can be created and sustained within firms and across networks of firms. However, for trust-based collaborative skill to become a true meta-capability, there must be investment not only within firms but also across society. Such investments will require a deep and sustained commitment, but there is evidence that societal investments do in fact pay off.

The Key Societal Challenge: Emphasizing and Investing in Collaborative Capability

Short-term, specifically targeted social investments have been shown to have a dramatic impact. For example, the United States invested heavily in the technical and managerial skills of women and minorities during World War II to build and maintain the capability for wartime production. Indeed, the production volume and efficiency of this rapidly developed workforce amazed even its proponents and contributed substantially to the Allied success in the war effort. After the war, the investments made in college and technical educations through the GI Bill were unprecedented in any advanced nation. Similarly, the investments made to rebuild the physical and social assets of Germany and Japan were enormous, as were their payoffs in terms of global prosperity and harmony. Those investments, coupled with the U.S. escape from the war without physical damage, created an economic strength and a managerial competence that attracted worldwide envy and imitation. We are still reaping the benefits of those investments, though today their value is seldom noted.

In recent decades, well-conceived investments have transformed the economies of many underdeveloped countries into powerful industrial producers. The quickly wrought economic transformations of South Korea, Singapore, and several Southeast Asian countries are dramatic demonstrations of the power of investments in human capital.

Ireland's economic development may well be the most informative example because it was so thoughtfully planned and targeted.[2] The Republic of Ireland in the post-war decades suffered because it had a narrow industrial base and a workforce with limited business skills. Moreover, the top graduates of Irish universities emigrated in large numbers in order to find outlets for their skills. In the last two decades of the twentieth century, Ireland's leaders took three bold steps to redirect economic development. First, they led the country into the European Union and established a free trade policy that clearly supported foreign investment. Second, they targeted computer software and customer service as underserved commercial markets in Europe. Third, they began a long-term program of European language training for Irish youth and young adults, along with training in software design and customer service.

The returns on these investments were visible within a decade. Firms from the United States and other countries established computer plants and distribution centers in Ireland, and the country rapidly became the center for flows of software to Europe and for service centers able to respond in all major languages. Unemployment dropped from over 20 percent to nearly 0, and workers from across Europe immigrated to Ireland. Many Irish nationals returned to contribute their skills to the new economy. Although the worldwide boom in information technology has slowed, the Irish economy still enjoys an unemployment rate of approximately 5 percent. The moral of the Ireland example, it seems to us, is that specific long-term economic capabilities can be developed rapidly and efficiently given intelligent policies and well-focused investments.

Removing Self-Imposed Barriers

The U.S. economy does not face the same set of challenges that were met by timely investments in infrastructure and human capital in the preceding examples. Clearly, the U.S. economy would benefit from increased human capital investments in scientific and technical education as well as additional investments in refurbishing the social infrastructure. However, the bigger investment challenges faced by the U.S. economy are those it is the least likely to make because they are constrained by what we have taught ourselves to believe about human behavior. That is, we have taught ourselves that it is natural and appropriate human behavior to pursue self-interest even if there are predictable social costs from such pursuit. Those social costs, which economists call externalities and military strategists refer to as collateral damage, are seldom given the same attention as profits and victories, and they result in greatly reduced benefits, if not actual losses, to society.

As long as we are captives of beliefs and teachings that management is responsible to only one stakeholder, the shareholders of firms, we will be tempted to pursue shortsighted strategies that ultimately erode and even destroy enterprise value. As long as we teach ourselves that opportunistic behavior is inevitable, we encourage the belief that it is pervasive and, in turn, we encourage massive investments aimed at its control. Clearly, whatever their investment costs, our teachings and beliefs about the inevitability of opportunistic behavior constrain our ability to benefit from knowledge sharing and collaborative value creation.

We believe that ultimately our society will overcome these largely self-imposed barriers. There is already enormous capacity around the world to build leadership competence in individuals and to develop team self-management skills. There is also a capacity, though smaller, to build competence in inter-firm collaboration and trust building. The current groundswell of public attention to corporate and social responsibility, and the growing pressure to thoroughly reexamine our priorities and beliefs, could lead to a broadened commitment to investments in these needed assets. A national commitment to social investments that create trust and collaborative capability—investments similar to those that helped create the meta-capabilities of coordination and delegation—would produce similar if not greater economic returns.

A Final Prediction

A new organizational form that allows firms to pursue strategies of continuous innovation is emerging. As this new form demonstrates its value, it will force the rethinking of current societal investment policies and help create a new business era characterized by collaborative values. Moreover, all of this will happen before we fully realize that it is even occurring.

Thirty or so years ago when we first began discussing with managers alternative market strategies and the different configurations of structures, capabilities, and managerial processes necessary to make those strategies work, many of them were still searching for the one best way of organizing. Today, virtually all managers recognize that healthy markets thrive on a mix of complementary strategies pursued by firms with capabilities and structures properly fitted to their chosen strategy.

Twenty-five years ago when we first explored with managers the potential value of forming flexible networks of firms arrayed along an industry's value chain, most managers were still convinced that vertical integration was essential to ensure quality control and operating efficiency. Today, numerous managers are confident of their ability to assemble inter-firm networks, complete with out-sourced functions and cooperative relationships, to deliver a new product or service.

Ten years ago when we suggested that self-managing teams might be one of the most effective mechanisms for coping with growing market and operating complexity, many managers were convinced that tighter central control was the only effective response to such complexity. Today, most managers recognize that hierarchical control usually slows decision times and distorts problem-solving information.

Five years ago, when we first started to describe collaborative multi-firm networks that might be able to pursue a continuous innovation strategy, most managers reacted much like the executive described in Chapter 7 who read our manuscript. They either dismissed the notion out of hand or raised one skeptical point after another in an effort to convince us that a network like OpWin's could not possibly work. Will such managerial attitudes toward multi-firm collaboration change, as have attitudes in the past?

Our most recent experiences with managers suggest that indeed their attitudes are changing. While most managers and firms probably are not yet ready to aggressively pursue the potential benefits of networks of firms that collaborate to both generate and share knowledge, experiments along these lines have already occurred, and supportive values and social investments are gaining public attention. Therefore, it is only a matter of time before a critical mass of managers fully embraces the ideas advanced here.

In fact, we expect, as has happened to us before, that we will someday find ourselves being shown around a highly successful firm engaged in multi-firm collaborative entrepreneurship by a manager who earlier had been adamantly opposed to the concept. Moreover, we expect that manager to casually comment on the firm's collaborative approach as, simply, "the way we do things here."

Reference Matter

Notes

Chapter 1

1. For a summary of our research on older organizational forms, as well as the newer network form of organizing, see Raymond E. Miles and Charles C. Snow, *Fit, Failure, and the Hall of Fame: How Companies Succeed or Fail* (New York: Free Press, 1994).

2. See Philipp A. W. Käser and Raymond E. Miles, "Understanding Knowledge Activists' Successes and Failures," *Long-Range Planning* 35 (2002): 9–28.

3. In the literature, complete packages of organizational resources usually are called configurations. See the Special Issue on Configurational Analysis of the *Academy of Management Journal*, December 1993. For a configuration to be fully operational, resources must be fitted together in a coherent fashion, and the entire configuration must fit its environment. See Raymond E. Miles and Charles C. Snow, "Fit, Failure, and the Hall of Fame," *California Management Review* 26, no. 3 (1984): 10–28. The original idea of a package or configuration of resources was presented by Edith A. Penrose, *The Theory of the Growth of the Firm* (London: Basil Blackwell, 1959). Penrose referred to the firm as a "bundle" of resources.

4. This is a very important point to keep in mind when designing or changing an organization. That is, a new type of organization cannot become fully operational until all of its major components—strategies, structures, capabilities, and management philosophies and processes—evolve to the proper stage. If even one component of the new package is better

suited for a different purpose, it will act as a constraint on the overall effectiveness of the new form. See Raymond E. Miles, Charles C. Snow, John A. Mathews, Grant Miles, and Henry J. Coleman, Jr., "Organizing in the Knowledge Age: Anticipating the Cellular Form," *Academy of Management Executive* 11, no. 4 (1997): 7–20.

5. For an example of how the teaching and learning process occurs across firms, see Zheng Zhao, Jaideep Anand, and Will Mitchell, "Transferring Collective Knowledge: Teaching and Learning in the Chinese Auto Industry," *Strategic Organization* 2, no. 2 (2004): 133–67.

Chapter 2

1. For discussions of how the concept of fit has been used in organizational research, see Raymond E. Miles and Charles C. Snow, "Fit, Failure, and the Hall of Fame," *California Management Review* 26, no. 3 (1984): 10–28; N. Venkatraman and John C. Camillus, "Exploring the Concept of 'Fit' in Strategic Management," *Academy of Management Review* 9 (1984): 513–25; N. Venkatraman, "The Concept of Fit in Strategy Research: Toward Verbal and Statistical Correspondence," *Academy of Management Review* 14 (1989): 423–44; and Prescott C. Ensign, "The Concept of Fit in Organizational Research," *International Journal of Organization Theory and Behavior* 4, no. 3 (2001): 287–306.

2. The importance of entrepreneurship and innovation to economic development was first discussed by Joseph A. Schumpeter in a book published in Germany in 1912. The English translation of his book is *The Theory of Economic Development: An Inquiry into Profits, Capital, Credit, Interest, and the Business Cycle* (Cambridge, MA: Harvard University Press, 1934). A recent empirical analysis came to exactly the same conclusion: Innovation is the primary cause of economic growth, and firm and interfirm ability to innovate explains why capitalist economies have much stronger growth records than other economic systems. See William J. Baumol, *The Free-Market Innovation Machine: Analyzing the Growth Miracle of Capitalism* (Princeton, NJ: Princeton University Press, 2002).

3. See Oliver Williamson, *Markets and Hierarchies: Analysis and Antitrust Implications* (New York: Free Press, 1975).

4. Ibid.

5. The multi-firm network organization was first described by Raymond E. Miles and Charles C. Snow, "Network Organizations: New Concepts for New Forms," *California Management Review* 28, no. 3 (1986): 62–73, and by Hans B. Thorelli, "Networks: Between Markets and Hierarchies," *Strategic Management Journal* 7 (1986): 37–51. Subsequently, ad-

ditional organizations such as various institutional actors, were included in the network concept. See W. P. Powell, "Neither Market Nor Hierarchy: Network Forms of Organization," *Research in Organizational Behavior* 12 (1990): 295–336, and "Inter-Organizational Collaboration in the Biotechnology Industry," *Journal of Institutional and Theoretical Economics* 151 (1996): 197–215.

6. Some observers have said that Peter Drucker's book *Concept of the Corporation* (New York: John Day, 1946) outlined the management and organizational blueprint for the entire second half of the twentieth century.

Chapter 3

1. For a detailed description of Corning's approach, see Margaret Graham and Alec Shuldner, *Corning and the Craft of Innovation* (New York: Oxford University Press, 2001).

2. For discussions of the relationship between corporate venturing and innovation, see Robert Burgelman and Leonard Sayles, *Inside Corporate Innovation* (New York: Free Press, 1986), and Zenas Block and Ian MacMillan, *Corporate Venturing* (Boston: Harvard Business School Press, 1993).

3. James A. Miles and J. Randall Woolridge, *Spin-Offs and Equity Carve-Outs: Achieving Faster Growth and Better Performance* (Morristown, NJ: Financial Executives Research Foundation, 1999).

4. Gary L. Lilien, Pamela D. Morrison, Kathleen Searls, Mary Sonnack, and Eric von Hippel, "Performance Assessment of the Lead User Idea-Generation Process for New Product Development," *Management Science* 48, no. 8 (2002): 1042–59.

5. Our discussion of continuous innovation is similar to the discussion of open innovation by Henry Chesbrough, *Open Innovation: The New Imperative for Creating and Profiting from Technology* (Boston: Harvard Business School Press, 2003), xxiv:

> Open Innovation is a paradigm that assumes that firms can and should use external ideas as well as internal ideas, and internal and external paths to market, as the firms look to advance their technology. Open Innovation combines internal and external ideas into architectures and systems whose requirements are defined by a business model. The business model utilizes both external and internal ideas to create value, while defining internal mechanisms to claim some portion of that value. Open Innovation assumes that internal ideas can also be taken to market through external channels, outside the current businesses of the firm, to generate additional value.

We agree that this new innovation paradigm will be highly attractive to many firms, but in addition, we want to emphasize that it is becoming increasingly feasible for innovation to be *continuous* and for it to occur *outside of a firm's traditional industry boundaries.*

6. Michael E. Porter popularized the concept of the value chain in his book *Competitive Advantage* (New York: Free Press, 1985).

7. For a description of how Dell Computer has created a virtual organization along its value chain, see Joan Magretta, "The Power of Virtual Integration: An Interview with Dell Computer's Michael Dell," *Harvard Business Review* 76 (1998): 73–84.

Chapter 4

1. Michael E. Porter has forcefully argued this position in *The Competitive Advantage of Nations* (New York: Free Press, 1990).

2. For a recent review of the literature on competitive dynamics, see David J. Ketchen, Jr., Charles C. Snow, and Vera L. Hoover, "Research on Competitive Dynamics: Recent Accomplishments and Future Challenges," *Journal of Management* 30, no. 6 (2004): 779–804.

3. The distinction between intrinsic and extrinsic motivation originally was drawn by psychologists such as Frederick Herzberg and Edward Deci. See Frederick Herzberg, *Work and the Nature of Man* (Cleveland, OH: World Publishing Company, 1966), and Edward L. Deci and Richard M. Ryan, *Intrinsic Motivation* (New York: Plenum Press, 1975).

4. For an overview of research and issues on trust in organizations, see Roderick M. Kramer and Tom R. Tyler, eds., *Trust in Organizations* (Thousand Oaks, CA: Sage, 1996).

5. By classifying participants' motives as mostly "self regarding" or "other regarding," Hector Rocha, Sumantra Ghoshal, and Lynda Gratton develop four different types of cooperation. See their working paper, "Beyond Self-Interest: Revisiting the Major Assumption in Economics and Management," London Business School, 2004. We believe that as participants' behavior becomes increasingly "other regarding," the closer it comes to what we call collaboration.

6. The classic "tit for tat" method of testing and calibration in cooperative relationships is described by Robert M. Axelrod, *The Evolution of Cooperation* (New York: Basic Books, 1984).

7. Raymond Noorda, founder and former CEO of Novell, Inc., coined the term *co-opetition* in the early 1990s. To better understand how co-opetition works, see Maria Bengtsson and Sorenson Kock, "'Coopetition' in Business Networks—To Cooperate and Compete Simultaneously," *Indus-

trial Marketing Management 29, no. 5 (2000): 411–26. For a description of the dynamics of co-opetition in the health care industry, see E. P. Gee, "Co-opetition: The New Market Milieu," *Journal of Healthcare Management* 45, no. 6 (2000): 359–63. For a discussion of how organizational characteristics affect co-opetition, see A. A. Lado, N. G. Boyd, and S. C. Hanlon, "Competition, Cooperation, and the Search for Economic Rents: A Syncretic Model," *Academy of Management Review* 22, no. 1 (1997): 110–41.

8. For a discussion of co-opetition from a game theoretic perspective, see A. M. Brandenberger and B. J. Nalebuff, *Co-opetition* (New York: Doubleday, 1996).

9. Our concept of collaborative entrepreneurship as a joint enterprise directed at the continuous creation of economic wealth was developed with Dr. Philipp A. W. Käser of the University of Zurich. Used in this way, our view of collaboration is very similar to that of D. G. Appley and A. E. Winder, "An Evolving Definition of Collaboration and Some Implications for the World of Work," *Journal of Applied Behavioral Science* 13, no. 3 (1977): 279–91. According to Appley and Winder, collaboration can only occur when certain conditions are present, such as voluntary relationships in which the parties care for and are committed to each other. Accordingly, we believe that collaboration as a joint enterprise will work best among competent, mature individuals who treat each other fairly and who value the relationship as much as their own self-interest.

10. For a discussion of the concept of caring trust, see Georg von Krogh, "Care in Knowledge Creation," *California Management Review* 40, no. 3 (1998): 133–53.

11. The concept of collaboration was first applied to organizations in the 1960s by Fred E. Emery and Eric Trist, "The Causal Texture of Organizational Environments," *Human Relations* 18 (1965): 21–32. Today, a notable arena in which collaborative knowledge sharing occurs across organizations is the biotechnology industry. See Walter W. Powell, K. W. Koput, and L. Smith-Doerr, "Interorganizational Cooperation and the Locus of Innovation: Networks of Learning in Biotechnology," *Administrative Science Quarterly* 41 (1996): 116–45. For a recent description of how collaboration works within an organization, see Leonard L. Berry, "The Collaborative Organization: Leadership Lessons from Mayo Clinic," *Organizational Dynamics* 33, no. 3 (2004): 228–42.

12. The notion that a perceived commitment to search for equitable returns is as important as the actual returns themselves has been supported empirically. Economists refer to this phenomenon as "procedural utility" (for a review of this literature, see Bruno S. Frey, Mathias Benz, and Alois

Stutzer, "Introducing Procedural Utility: Not Only What but Also How Matters," *Journal of Institutional and Theoretical Economics*, forthcoming). One study found that corporate and individual litigants involved in federal court-ordered arbitrations were much more likely to accept the arbitrated awards, irrespective of the actual outcomes, if they perceived the arbitration process as fair. See E. Allan Lind, Carol T. Kulik, Maureen Ambrose, and Maria V. de Vera Park, "Individual and Corporate Dispute Resolution: Using Procedural Fairness as a Decision Heuristic," *Administrative Science Quarterly* 38, no. 2 (1993): 224–51.

13. For an account of Linux's origin and development, see E. S. Raymond, "The Cathedral and the Bazaar: Musings on Linux and Open Source by an Accidental Revolutionary," in C. DiBona, S. Ockman, and M. Stone, *Open Sources: Voices from the Open Source Revolution* (Sebastopol, CA: O'Reilly and Associates, 1999). Linux's recent status is described in Steve Hamm, "LINUXINC," *Business Week* (January 31, 2005): 60–68.

14. For a description of how Linux and other Internet technologies are regulated, see Sirkka L. Jarvenpaa, Emerson Tiller, and Robert Simons, "Regulation and the Internet: Public Choice Insights for Business Organizations," *California Management Review* 46, no. 1 (2003): 72–85.

15. The community of creation model is described by Mohanbir Sawhney and Emanuela Prandelli, "Communities of Creation: Managing Distributed Innovation in Turbulent Markets," *California Management Review* 42, no. 4 (2000): 24–54. Communities of practice are discussed by E. Wenger, *Communities of Practice: Learning, Meaning, and Identity* (New York: Cambridge University Press, 1998).

16. For a description of the information technology industry in Finland, see Kirsimarja Blomqvist, "Partnering in the Dynamic Environment: The Role of Trust in Asymmetric Technology Partnership Formation," Ph.D. Dissertation, Lappeenranta University of Technology (Finland), 2002.

17. For a discussion of inter-firm alliances in Southeast Asia, along with their supporting institutional policies and mechanisms, see John A. Mathews and Dong-Sung Cho, *Tiger Technology: The Creation of a Semiconductor Industry in East Asia* (Cambridge, England: Cambridge University Press, 2000).

18. Kirsimarja Blomqvist, "The Role and Means of Trust Creation in Partnership Formation Between Small and Large Technology Firms: A Preliminary Study of How Small Firms Attempt to Create Trust in Their Potential Partners," in Wim During and Ray Oakey, eds., *New Technology-Based Firms in the 1990s*, Vol. IV (London: Paul Chapman Publishing, 1998).

19. Our argument that European culture is highly suited to commercial

forms of collaboration is fully developed by Jeremy Rifkin, *The European Dream: How Europe's Vision of the Future Is Quietly Eclipsing the American Dream* (New York: Penguin, 2004). Rifkin says that Europe's flexible, communitarian model of society, business, and citizenship can meet the challenges of the twenty-first century.

20. Siv Vangen and Chris Huxham, "Nurturing Collaborative Relations: Building Trust in Inter-organizational Collaboration," *Journal of Applied Behavioral Science* 39, no. 1 (2003): 5–31. For a theoretical discussion of the relationships among collaboration, social networks, and innovation, see Philipp A. W. Käser, "Tie Strength and Tie Dynamic: New Relationships and Realities," paper presented at the EGOS Conference, 2004.

21. For examples of organizations that use a meta-capability of collaboration as a source of competitive advantage, see Jeanne M. Liedtka, "Collaborating Across Lines of Business for Competitive Advantage," *Academy of Management Executive* 10, no. 2 (1996): 20–34.

Chapter 5

1. For a detailed description of Intel Corporation's external research efforts, see Chesbrough, *Open Innovation*, Chapter 6. For additional examples of external venturing, see Henry Chesbrough, "Making Sense of Corporate Venture Capital," *Harvard Business Review* 80, no. 3 (2002): 90–99.

2. The Boeing Company uses a similar approach for its SLICE team. This team uses an Internet notebook and project vault to store information and provide secure access to team members, no matter where they are located. Security is critical because many team members are not Boeing employees but rather come from external organizations to provide their expertise on a project. See the American Productivity and Quality Center's 2002 Best Practice Report (Using Knowledge Management to Drive Innovation) and its 2004 Best Practice Report (Virtual Collaboration: Enabling Project Teams and Communities).

3. All of NetAge's products and services can be found on the Web at *http://www.virtualteams.com*.

4. TCG's triangulation strategy is discussed in John A. Mathews, "TCG R&D Networks: The Triangulation Strategy," *Journal of Industry Studies* 1 (1993): 65–74.

5. The VAIC system was developed by Ante Pulic and his colleagues at the Austrian Intellectual Capital Research Center. For a description, see Leif Edvinsson, *Corporate Longitude: What You Need to Know to Navigate the Knowledge Economy* (London: Prentice Hall, 2002), Chapter 2.

Chapter 6

1. Noel Brings Jacobsen and Stefan Anderberg, "The Evolution of Industrial Symbiotic Networks—The Case of Kalundborg," paper presented at the ISIE Conference in Leiden, The Netherlands, November 12–14, 2001.

2. See "Partnering: A Concept for Success," Associated General Contractors of America, September 1991, and "P2 Partnering Plus: Working Together," Texas Department of Transportation, Continuous Improvement Office, December 1996.

3. For an overview of Acer's business philosophy and organizational approach, see John A. Mathews and Charles C. Snow, "A Conversation with Taiwan-Based Acer Group's Stan Shih on Global Strategy and Management," *Organizational Dynamics* 27, no. 1 (1998): 65–74. For other examples of collaborative international alliances, see John A. Mathews, *Dragon Multinational: A New Model of Global Growth* (New York: Oxford University Press, 2002).

4. Our notion that knowledge-sharing collaboration can become an organizational process or routine that is teachable to others is very similar to the Japanese concept of *kata*, a continuous dialectical process that is second nature to the organization. See Ikujiro Nonaka and Patrick Reinmoellor, "Knowledge Creation and Utilization: Promoting Dynamic Systems of Creative Routines," in M. A. Hitt, R. Amit, C. E. Lucier, and R. D. Nixon, eds., *Creating Value: Winners in the New Business Environment* (Oxford: Blackwell Publishing, 2002), 104–28.

5. Such an inter-organizational learning process has been described in a different region, that of Ålesund, Norway. See Jon Hanssen-Bauer and Charles C. Snow, "Responding to Hypercompetition: The Structure and Processes of a Regional Learning Network Organization," *Organization Science* 7 (1996): 413–27. The learning model used by this regional network has five stages: information acquisition, interpretation, focused experimentation, diffusion of experience, and restructuring of knowledge.

6. Charles E. Cowan, "Partnering in Fixed-Price Contracts—A New Paradigm," Working Paper, January 1990. This paper describes the first partnering experiment in the construction industry.

7. Holding workshops to build relationships and trust at the beginning of projects has now achieved the status of best practice. See American Productivity and Quality Center, 2002 Best Practice Report (Using Knowledge Management to Drive Innovation).

8. Link-and-leverage strategies used by latecomer multinational firms are discussed in United Nations Industrial Development Organization

(UNIDO), *Industrial Development Report 2002* (Vienna, Austria: United Nations, 2002). For a theoretical development of latecomer firms in terms of resource leverage, see John A. Mathews, "The Competitive Advantages of the Latecomer Firm: A Resource-Based Perspective," *Asia-Pacific Journal of Management* 19 (2002): 467–88.

Chapter 7

1. In his book *The Human Organization: Its Management and Value* (New York: McGraw-Hill, 1967), Rensis E. Likert referred to his approach as human asset accounting. Now referred to more broadly as knowledge management, this approach includes (a) managing information (explicit, recorded knowledge), (b) managing processes (embedded knowledge), (c) managing people (tacit knowledge), (d) managing innovation (knowledge conversion), and (e) managing intangible assets (intellectual capital). See Edvinsson, *Corporate Longitude*, page 15, footnote 7. Edvinsson's book also presents a timeline of key knowledge management developments (pages 13–15). We predict that eventually firms will calculate and report their investments in, and benefits from, various intangible assets such as organizational capabilities, brand identities, patents and know-how, and networks of professional and business relationships. The frameworks and methods for doing so can be found in John R. M. Hand and Baruch Lev, eds., *Intangible Assets: Values, Measures, and Risks* (New York: Oxford University Press, 2003); the Brookings Institution's two-part report, *Project on Understanding Intangible Sources of Value* (Washington, DC: Brookings Institution, 2000); and Baruch Lev, "Sharpening the Intangibles Edge," *Harvard Business Review* 82, no. 6 (2004): 109–16. For an excellent theoretical discussion of all these matters using the construct of social capital, see Paul S. Adler and Seok-Woo Kwon, "Social Capital: Prospects for a New Concept," *Academy of Management Review* 27, no. 1 (2002): 17–40.

2. The government of Denmark published the first guidelines for intellectual capital accounting in 2000. See Edvinsson, *Corporate Longitude*, page 15.

3. The classic statement of corporate governance using an agency perspective is Michael C. Jensen and William H. Meckling, "Theory of the Firm: Managerial Behavior, Agency Costs, and Ownership Structure," *Journal of Financial Economics* 3 (1976): 305–60. For a discussion of the issues in the current corporate governance debate, see the symposium "Challenges to Corporate Governance," *Law and Contemporary Problems* 62, no. 3 (1999).

4. Probably the most accessible treatment of this issue is Alfred D. Chandler, Jr., *The Visible Hand: The Managerial Revolution in American Business* (Cambridge, MA: Belknap Press of Harvard University Press, 1977).

5. The classic book on industrial organization economics is Joseph Bain, *Industrial Organization* (New York: Wiley, 1959). The path-breaking discussion of oligopoly theory is Edward H. Chamberlin, *The Theory of Monopolistic Competition* (Cambridge, MA: Harvard University Press, 1933).

6. One popular article that made this point is Michael E. Porter, "From Competitive Advantage to Corporate Strategy," *Harvard Business Review* 65, no. 3 (1987): 43–59.

7. The original portfolio approach was developed by the Boston Consulting Group. See Bruce Henderson, *The Product Portfolio* (Boston: Boston Consulting Group, 1970). The logic of this approach is still widely used today.

8. Peter J. Buckley and Mark C. Casson, *The Future of the Multinational Enterprise* (London: Holmes & Meier, 1976).

9. The origin of this theoretical perspective can be traced to Edith A. Penrose, *The Theory of the Growth of the Firm* (London: Basil Blackwell, 1959). The two most-often cited articles on the resource-based view are Birger Wernerfelt, "A Resource-Based View of the Firm," *Strategic Management Journal* 5, no. 2 (1984): 795–15, and Jay Barney, "Firm Resources and Sustained Competitive Advantage," *Journal of Management* 17 (1991): 99–120.

10. The concept of firm capability was popularized as core competencies by C. K. Prahalad and Gary Hamel, "The Core Competence of the Corporation," *Harvard Business Review* 68 (May–June 1990): 79–91.

11. David J. Teece, Gary Pisano, and Amy Shuen, "Dynamic Capabilities and Strategic Management," *Strategic Management Journal* 18 (1997): 509–33.

12. For a recent discussion of knowledge management issues and approaches, see Eric Lesser and Laurence Prusak, eds., *Creating Value with Knowledge* (New York: Oxford University Press, 2003).

13. Probably the best source for locating these various competitive strategies is the leading strategic management textbook: Arthur A. Thompson, Jr., A. J. Strickland, III, and John Gamble, *Crafting and Executing Strategy: The Quest for Competitive Advantage*, 14th ed. (New York: McGraw-Hill/Irwin, 2004).

14. For a review, see Jeffrey Dyer, *Collaborative Advantage* (New York: Oxford University Press, 2000).

15. The most recent study of the so-called management effect is by

Timothy W. Ruefli and Robert R. Wiggins, "Industry, Corporate, and Segment Effects, and Business Performance: A Non-Parametric Approach," *Strategic Management Journal* 24, no. 9 (2003): 861–79. According to this study, corporate factors explain firm performance much more than do industry factors, indicating that managers' decisions and actions have considerably more influence on a firm's performance than does the industry in which the firm exists.

16. Not all theories portray organizations as adaptive mechanisms guided by the decisions of managers. However, we agree with Sumantra Ghoshal and Peter Moran that such deterministic perspectives are essentially wrong and unhelpful. See their article, "Bad for Practice: A Critique of the Transaction Cost Theory," *Academy of Management Review* 21, no. 1 (1996): 13–47.

17. The needed tools and reporting frameworks are available, but firms are not yet required by law to use them. Some firms, such as Skandia Insurance, voluntarily calculate and report investments in intangible assets because they find it managerially helpful. We believe that this practice will begin to spread among other firms. For a discussion of the issues, see Hand and Lev, *Intangible Assets*, especially Chapters 17–20.

18. For a discussion of the broader set of human motives that can and should operate in organizations, see Hector O. Rocha and Sumantra Ghoshal, "Beyond Self-Interest: Revisiting the Major Assumption in Economics and Management," Working Paper, London Business School, 2004.

Chapter 8

1. The assumption that trust and predictability can be created through investments in the development of protocols, and in the orientation and training needed to help new firms use them effectively, is crucial to the success of the OpWin model. The literature on social networks, now being applied to organizational interactions, suggests that there is a tradeoff between having a few close relationships that generate predictability and trust and having a broader array of weaker linkages that could provide a more diverse source of new knowledge. However, if a broad group of diverse and even geographically distant firms can develop OpWin-like trust through protocol building and training, then they can enjoy the benefits of *both* rich knowledge-sharing opportunities and close relationships. For a recent summary of social network designs and benefits, see Daniel J. Brass, Joseph Galaskiewicz, Henrich R. Greve, and Wenpin Tsai, Guest Coeditors, Special Research Forum on Building Effective Networks, *Academy of Management Journal* 47, no. 6 (2004): 795–906.

2. See American Productivity and Quality Center, 2004 Best Practice Report (Virtual Collaboration: Enabling Project Teams and Communities).

Chapter 9

1. Shoshana Zuboff, "The Morphing of Capitalism," from "A Call to Action," *Fast Company* 5, no. 1 (January 14, 2004), and "You Say You Want a Revolution," *Fast Company* 5, no. 6 (April 7, 2004).

2. For an account of Ireland's national policies, social investments, and achievements, see Dennis O'Hearn, *Inside the Celtic Tiger: The Irish Economy and the Asian Model* (London: Pluto Press, 1998).

Resource Guide on Collaborative Entrepreneurship

This Resource Guide is designed to help you locate resources on key aspects of collaborative entrepreneurship. It is not a comprehensive listing of resources but rather a means of getting you started in your search for the specific resources that you need. For each topic, we provide three types of resources: (1) a classic statement of the subject drawn from the organizational literature, (2) recent books on the topic, and (3) Web sites that you can visit for ideas and further guidance.

Collaboration and Entrepreneurial Community

Classic Statement

D. G. Appley and A. E. Winder, "An Evolving Definition of Collaboration and Some Implications for the World of Work," *Journal of Applied Behavioral Science* 13, no. 3 (1977): 279–91.

Recent Books

Jeffrey Dyer, *Collaborative Advantage* (New York: Oxford University Press, 2000).

Jessica Lipnack and Jeffrey Stamps, *Virtual Teams: Reaching Across Space, Time, and Organizations with Technology*, rev. ed. (New York: Wiley, 2001).

Web Sites

http://edwardlowe.org/build1.shtm1#regional   An article on the various factors required to build an entrepreneurial community from the Edward Lowe Foundation.

http://www.icansi.com/overview.html   The Web site of the International Center for Alliances, Networks, and Strategic Innovation, a global community of researchers and practitioners concerned with the development and utilization of alliances.

http://ncoe.org   The National Commission on Entrepreneurship, based in Washington, DC, provides local, state, and national leaders with a roadmap for sustaining and expanding a flourishing entrepreneurial economy.

http://thealliancedworld.com/index.html   A portal dedicated to key aspects of strategic alliances. Includes information on alliance strategy, fundamentals, and performance metrics.

Intangible Asset Valuation and Accounting

Classic Statement

Rensis E. Likert, *The Human Organization: Its Management and Value* (New York: McGraw-Hill, 1967).

Recent Books

Stan Davis and Christopher Meyer, *Future Wealth* (Boston: Harvard Business School Press, 2000).

John R. M. Hand and Baruch Lev, eds., *Intangible Assets: Values, Measures, and Risks* (New York: Oxford University Press, 2003).

Baruch Lev, *Intangibles: Management, Measurement, and Reporting* (Washington, DC: Brookings Institution Press, 2001).

Web Sites

http://bvfls.aicpa.org/Resources/Business+Valuation/Valuing+an+Intangible+Asset/   Information on intangible asset valuation from the American Institute of Certified Public Accountants.

http://www.intangiblebusiness.com/home.asp   A London-based firm
that offers brand valuation services. The site contains recent news on
market research and brand valuation, and it is a good case example
of how to value a brand as an intangible asset.
*http://www.valuationresources.com/Publications/IntangiblePubDesc/
Intangible.htm*   A list of recent publications dealing with intangible
asset valuation.

Intrinsic Motivation

Classic Statement

Edward L. Deci and Richard M. Ryan, *Intrinsic Motivation* (New York:
Plenum Press, 1975).

Recent Books

Bruno S. Frey and Margit Osterloh, eds., *Successful Management by
Motivation* (Berlin: Springer-Verlag, 2002).

Web Sites

http://www.hrgopher.com   Provides links to online resources across all
human resource areas. See the link Motivation, Recognition, and
Awards.
http://www.motivation-club.com/entrepreneur_motivation.html
A summary of practical advice relating to entrepreneurial
motivation.
http://www.themanager.org/Knowledgebase/HR/Motivation.htm
Contains a wide range of classic and more recent writings on
measuring, managing, and understanding employee motivation.

Knowledge Management and Innovation

Classic Statement

Ikujiro Nonaka and H. Takeuchi, *The Knowledge-Creating Company:
How Japanese Companies Create the Dynamics of Innovation*
(New York: Oxford University Press, 1995).

Recent Books

Henry Chesbrough, *Open Innovation: The New Imperative for Creating and Profiting from Technology* (Boston: Harvard Business School Press, 2003).

Leif Edvinsson, *Corporate Longitude: What You Need to Know to Navigate the Knowledge Economy* (London: Prentice Hall, 2002).

Leif Edvinsson and Michael Malone, *Intellectual Capital: Realizing Your Company's True Value by Finding Its Hidden Brainpower* (New York: HarperBusiness, 1997).

Eric Lesser and Laurence Prusak, eds., *Creating Value with Knowledge* (New York: Oxford University Press, 2003).

Web Sites

http://www.breakthroughdiscoveries.org/index.asp   Alliances for Discovery is a network of organizations and individuals that has the collaborative goal of facilitating 100 breakthrough discoveries over the next ten years.

http://www.innovationtools.com/   Offers a number of easily understandable tools, strategies, and techniques for creativity and innovation. Key topics include enterprise innovation, mind mapping, idea management, and brainstorming.

http://www.Knexa.com   This site facilitates the exchange and trade of knowledge assets globally. Based in Vancouver, British Columbia, Knexa is pioneering the concept of the knowledge exchange auction. It is one of the first exchanges in the world where users can buy and sell their knowledge and experience online.

http://www.KnowledgeBoard.com   An online community to create a global exchange of knowledge management expertise and interest. European in its focus.

http://www.knowledgebusiness.com   A global community of knowledge-driven organizations dedicated to networking, benchmarking, and sharing best practices leading to superior performance.

http://www.knowledgepoint.com.au/   A site with a number of articles on knowledge management, business intelligence, information management, and intellectual capital.

http://www.wipo.int   The site of the World Intellectual Property Organization. Contains information on a wide variety of intellectual property issues.

Network and Self-Managing Organizations

Classic Statement

Raymond E. Miles and Charles C. Snow, "Network Organizations:
New Concepts for New Forms," *California Management Review* 28,
no. 3 (1986): 62–73.

Walter W. Powell, "Neither Market nor Hierarchy: Network Forms of
Organization," *Research on Organizational Behavior* 12 (1990):
295–336.

Hans B. Thorelli, "Networks: Between Markets and Hierarchies,"
Strategic Management Journal 7 (1986): 37–51.

Recent Books

Albert-Laszlo Barabasi, *Linked: How Everything Is Connected to
Everything Else and What It Means for Business, Science, and
Everyday Life* (New York: Plume, 2003).

Manuel Castells, *The Information Age: Economy, Society, and
Culture* (Oxford: Blackwell Publishing, 1996). See especially Vol. I
(*The Rise of the Network Society*).

Michael Goold and Andrew Campbell, *Designing Effective Organizations: How to Create Structured Networks* (New York: Wiley,
2002).

Christine Parker, *The Open Corporation: Effective Self-Regulation and
Democracy* (London: Cambridge University Press, 2002).

Ilkka Tuomi, *Networks of Innovation* (New York: Oxford University
Press, 2002).

Web Sites

http://www.businessofgovernment.org   This is the site of the IBM
Center for the Business of Government. It provides cutting-edge
knowledge to government leaders on topics such as network
organizations, collaborative alliances, and knowledge
management.

http://www.ve-forum.org/   A portal focused on network organizations
and virtual collaboration. The Virtual Enterprise Forum is a
community of consultants, practitioners, researchers, and
technologists.

The following sites contain specific information about virtual teams:

http://www.mapnp.org/library/grp_sk11/virtual/virtual.htm   A site that provides information on the composition, management, and leadership of virtual teams.

http://www.skyrme.com/resource/virtres.htm   Contains a list of online resources and publications in the areas of virtual organizations and teleworking. Good concise reviews presented in layman's language.

http://www.startwright.com/virtual.htm   A wide-ranging list of online resources, links, and articles on virtual teams.

http://www.virtualteams.com   This site contains books on network organizations and virtual teams, including a model of how teams can collaborate within and across firms.

Trust and Trust-Building

Classic Statement

Bernard Barber, *The Logic and Limits of Trust* (New Brunswick, NJ: Rutgers University Press, 1974).

Recent Books

Ronald S. Burt, *Trust, Reputation and Competitive Advantage* (New York: Oxford University Press, 2005).

Roderick M. Kramer and Tom R. Tyler, eds., *Trust in Organizations* (Thousand Oaks, CA: Sage, 1996).

Robert C. Solomon and Fernando Flores, *Building Trust in Business, Politics, Relationships, and Life* (New York: Oxford University Press, 2003).

Web Sites

http://www.intractableconflict.org/m/trust_building.jsp   An article on interpersonal trust building and links to online and offline resources concerning trust.

http://www.librarysupportstaff.com/coworkers2.html   Articles and online links to material on building trust in the workplace and the role of trust in organizations.

http://www.1000ventures.com/business_guide/crosscuttings/ relationships_trust.html   A collection of books, articles, and other resources and links on building trust between individuals and organizations.

http://www.wilsonweb.com/wmt6/start-trust.htm   A specific example that offers some useful tips on establishing customer trust via a company Web site.

Index